I0518490

When Orchids Speak

Speak

The True Nature of Reality

Marlene St. Joan Moulton, M.D.

For more information, please contact:

Marlene S. Moulton, M.D.

The Listening Doctor PLLC

www.thelisteningdoctor.com

Info@thelisteningdoctor.com

Ebook ISBN: 979-8-9996736-2-6

Hardcover ISBN: 979-8-9996736-1-9

Paperback ISBN: 979-8-9996736-0-2

Dedication

I dedicate this book, first and foremost, to my daughter Rochelle; a powerful and always moving energy who came into this world, into this universe, and into this lifetime to share these experiences with me. Experiences that made me better, stronger, and wiser. Rochelle, you have played your role in every way possible, and I would love to thank you for that.

To my grandchildren, Landon Levi Campbell and Serenity Sapphire Campbell, I want you to remember that the experiences you shared with me are ones that allowed you to experience this world as a hologram. Use this book as a frame of reference, and as a reminder in the future when the time comes for you to develop your own experience in this holographic world.

To my husband, Richard, my angel here on earth, your role has always been to remind me to stay centered. I thank you so much for being a part of my soul group, and for loving me despite my quirks.

To my Aunt Veda, without you, there would be no me. I love you, and I thank you with all my heart and soul.

Foreword

In a world shaped by familiar narratives and shared assumptions, encountering a voice like Marlene's is a rare and stirring experience. Her journey—woven through moments of clarity, confusion, resilience, and revelation—offers a window into a life lived with deep introspection. Through her conscious reflections and unconscious musings, Marlene challenges us to reconsider what we think we know about identity, purpose, and the quiet truths that shape our days.

This book is not an endorsement of a singular worldview, but an invitation to witness one woman's path with empathy and curiosity. As I read, I found myself less concerned with agreement and more captivated by understanding. I hope you, too, will find wonder in these pages— wonder at the courage it takes to share one's inner world, and at the unexpected ways it might echo within your own.

- Richard Dave Moulton

Table of Contents

Preface

We are deeply immersed in a holographic game called life. The problem is, no one taught us the rules of the game. The original intention of the game was collecting information through education, but over time we were forced to fight for the freedom of our Souls. A series of events happened in my life that led to my own self-discovery. It revealed an independent Divine conscious energy within my body; my Soul.

Notice I did not say "I read." Let me be very clear, I have *lived* these experiences unaided by drugs, be it plant based or manufactured, illicit or prescribed. I discovered that the world is an interactive digital hologram made up of energy and light materialized as matter. Through a process we call "spiritual awakening," what was once magic, we now call psionics. Endowed with this ability through repeated out of body experiences, astral travels, inter-dimensional shifts, and interactions with inter-dimensional beings, have all allowed me to better see and understand the world as a construct. It's one that creates the illusion of matter via a play of light and darkness. These experiences also allowed me to witness myself as a projection of the Divine source, positioned beyond the void of infinite pure consciousness. My journeys led to an unexpected self-discovery and subsequent deconstruction of my prior illusions. I was granted access to see the world as it truly operates. It is, however, impossible to go through something that life-changing and not share it, even to the detriment of self. This is what led me to want to share my story.

I had no initial plans of writing this book. But every time I verbally shared my story with a patient, family, or a friend, they all said the same thing, "You should write a book." Even as I maneuvered my daily life, every time I got to the stop light at the intersection of Daniel's Parkway and Six Miles Cypress, I heard my Soul say, "Marlene, the book." So, I finally gave in. I felt my higher self sitting on my left shoulder witnessing the unfolding. With that came a series of automatic writing that eventually became this very book. Every word flowed effortlessly through me. These psionic experiences convinced me that this is a part of our humanness and that we all have a divine story to tell, whether on this side of reality or the next. Remember I told you so.

This interactive Universe is delivering a message through me, one that I wish to share with you. As you accompany me, I ask not for your belief, but for you to keep an open mind, and remain honest with yourself about the parts of my journey that may resonate with you.

As we begin, I will first explore my fascinating, exhilarating interactive journey through the Universe that led to my own self-discovery. From there, I will share the lessons I learned about this game called life, culminating in a message from the inter-dimensional beings. When my innate instinct to search for a deeper meaning of life was ignited, the things that meet the eye, as life and living, crumbled. I began a journey where intellect met intuition, and, as a result, intellect was ultimately shattered. As I watched myth meet reality, my life became a cross between *Alice in Wonderland* and *Star Wars*. Here is my journey to the Divine source within me.

Chapter 1:

THE BIRTH OF SELF

They say hindsight is twenty-twenty, but looking back at my role in this game called life, I can clearly see how the Universe orchestrated my arrival. The very dance of my creation had been set into motion, and was playing out with or without my full awareness.

At a very early age, I subconsciously understood my agreement with the Divine, and though the road to recognizing this was not easy, I knew that to fully play out this role, I was going to become a doctor. With greater inner-knowledge, I can appreciate the convoluted orchestration of my life, and my interaction with the fabric that binds the ether and spacetime. Nothing on this path was by chance; it took an entire village to raise me and the entire Universe to awake me. My current life path is as a result of every one-off person who popped in to make something happen along the way. Those who existed simply to spark a memory, or the ones whose presence and force created beautiful or even traumatic memories; they all changed the course of my actions in this game. Some players and forces remained steadfast in my life and became stable rocks upon which the foundation of the illusion of my game called life was created.

Though I lay myself bare as I share this journey with you, I ask that you walk with me as I paint a picture of my path, and allow me to present myself as a rational, scientific, and highly functioning member of this society. This detail is very important as the incredulous stories I am about to share with you will leave you with many questions. Through stories of miracles and magic, armed with bravery and curiosity, I walked the line between genius and madness. Each new experience is more exhilarating than the one before. What I am about to share might be attributed to God, spirituality or mysticism. I attribute it to science. I am convinced that this is a merger between spirituality and science. It is a shame that our conversations about our humanness does not involve and support both arms of this existence. I have no apologies, and shamelessly share with you my high strangeness. I am convinced that one day science will catch up with the finer elements that support my experiences. Until then, I want to leave my personal experience in my own words as a contribution to that future process. Maybe something in the way I explain these experiences will ring true and contribute to future scientific discoveries about our humanness. Honestly, I hesitated in sharing this deeply personal journey with you, then I thought, the fearless person that I am, who better to tell you this wild tale, if not me?

You see, the identity I assumed at birth was born in Jamaica to a beautiful twenty-three-year-old woman named Elsa. My father, who I lovingly refer to as my sperm donor, was a well-known Jamaican reggae artist named George Linton Brown, or as he was known to his fans, Jackie

Brown. But to better understand me, as well as my generational and spiritual karma, I must first introduce you to my lineage.

My paternal great-great-grandmother was a Maroon, a group of Indigenous Jamaicans who were captured and enslaved during the British invasion. Eventually escaping captivity, she, along with several other slaves, retreated to and inhabited the high mountains of Portland. As part of a rebel group who single-handedly fought back against the British in a revolution, their efforts led to the independence of the island of Jamaica. Maroon Town is named after these brave men and women, and my grandmother, Loretta Brown, was a descendant of this tribe. She was a loving, highly intuitive woman whom I met later in my life. She gave birth to my father, George Linton, who, in his own right, was a mystic and creative Soul. He named me Marlene St. Joan Brown.

On the other hand, my maternal great-grandmother, Letitia Solomon, who was born in 1825, and returned to the stars in 1935, was a strong, beautiful woman from Surinam. Known for her petite stature, she, too, found herself enslaved by the British, and was later sold into the slave trade to a Jamaican plantation owner. There, she met and married James Miller Chambers. As her family matriarch, she raised her children, and lived to the ripe age of one hundred and ten years old. Her daughter, Jane Chambers, married Joshua Smith, and together, the couple gave birth to my mother Elsa.

My maternal grandparents, Joshua and Jane Smith, farmers in Saint Elizabeth, Jamaica, had nine children; seven boys and two girls. Jane died when my mother was around fifteen years old, and my Aunt Veda, her youngest sister, was only seven years old. After her death, the family was raised by grandfather Joshua, who instilled a strong sense of education in

5

his children. For each child, upon graduating from high-school, he offered them a boat ticket to England. Child after child, he used the hard-earned money he earned from farming to shuttle them off to Europe, in hopes of them gaining a better education. From their first son to Elsa, my mother, every child was given this opportunity. All except my Aunt Veda. After graduating high-school, Aunt Veda was denied the opportunity to study abroad as her father needed someone to remain at home to assist him with running his household.

When my grandfather suddenly died from a stroke, my mother, who was only twenty years old, was now an orphan along with all her siblings. Prior to his death, my mother had been offered the opportunity to migrate to England to further her education. But rather than join her brothers, she chose to remain at home after falling in love with a man named Mack.

He was a violent man whose verbal and physical abuse caused my mother to suffer several miscarriages. She was finally rescued by her sister, my Aunt Veda, and her brother, my Uncle Roy, who took her to live with them in Kingston, Jamaica. Though married to Mack at the time, it was then that my mother met and fell in love with my father. Soon after they met, she gave birth to my brother Michael, followed by me. It is through this long ancestral African lineage, filled with energy in motion and karma, that I descended into this game called life.

My parents' relationship did not last long. Nine years after separating from her husband, and shortly after giving birth to me, her abusive husband came knocking. Without hesitation, she packed her things and returned to him with me in tow. Time would quickly reveal that I was not welcome in his home.

My brother Michael, my parents' first child, whom my father loved deeply, was left behind to be with him. While there, however, he would often find himself in the middle of my father's relationship problems with his new, jealous lover. One summer, the woman sent my brother across a busy highway by himself to run an errand. As he attempted to cross, he was struck by a car, dying instantly from a broken neck, and multiple head injuries. He was only eight years old. Though I was four years old at the time, at his funeral, I recall touching his lifeless body as I tried to understand why my brother was not moving while I still saw him alive above himself. Someone eventually got hold of me and removed me from the casket.

When my mother went back to her husband, I was unhappy there. At only three-months-old, I still have vivid memories of me as a baby, laying on my back crying until my entire body shook in what felt like tremors. But whenever Aunt Veda came to visit us, and held me in her arms, I would feel so loved that it was the only time I would not cry.

I called this the "Moses down the river" part of my life. In my mother's attempt to save her own Soul, and possibly mine, she gave me away to her sister. Her sacrifice would give birth to separation anxiety within me, a condition I suffered with for a long time before its eventual release. Separation anxiety was my first childhood trauma. It was not until I became a fully practicing medical professional, and after self-diagnosis that I was able to recognize the initiation and release of this disease.

In hindsight, separation anxiety manifested itself in many ways in my life. Throughout my childhood, Aunt Veda was never able to leave me alone. I loved her dearly, but I understand that I held on as tightly as I did because she was my one safe place. I knew that on Earth she was the only human in the flesh I had, and I could not lose her.

Veda Maude Smith, the woman of great maternal instinct, unfortunately had no children of her own. Plagued with fibroids, she had a hysterectomy when I was about nine years old, and was never able to get pregnant. It is almost as if the universe knew I was to be her child.

I sometimes tell myself that this was why she was denied the opportunity to go to England, and why she had no children of her own. Through my mother's sacrifice, I became her child, but she became the cornerstone of my life. The trauma of separation—the realities of its existence and the possibilities of its recurrence—shaped my life.

Because of this anxiety, by the time I was seven years old, I felt like I did not belong anywhere. I did not fit into a structured family, and I could not shake the sense that I came from some other place. Although I loved my Aunt Veda and Uncle Roy, I was aware of a deep inner longing for a love and reunion with someone or something I knew that was not of this world. Although I could not identify the source, I knew that they were not earthly. The longing for their presence in my life felt unquenchable. The separation anxiety brewing in me became the trigger that unknowingly forced me to begin seeking my Soul. Needless to say, my journey to my Soul began early in life.

Chapter 2:

EARLY EDUCATION

Growing up means living, and through life comes an education, formal or informal. Aunt Veda found different ways to teach me; reading to me long before I could read to myself. She bought a series of books about Bible stories and would read to me every day after dinner. The first series we read together began with stories about Jesus, Moses, Jacob, and other characters I now cannot recall. As she read these stories aloud to me each day, I fell in love with Jesus and believed that He might be my person.

At just five years old, the story of Jesus' life resonated with me. The more I learned about Him, the more I felt a part of me still sleeping deep within begin to stir. As Aunt Veda read stories of Jesus being a fisherman, working in carpentry, or going into a temple and turning over the tables, I was hooked. I saw Jesus as a rebel with a cause, and admired the way He stood up for truth. I saw principles in Him that I wanted to one day emulate. But, of all the things Jesus had done as a carpenter and fisherman, it was His acts of healing that came through to me.

When reading one night, Aunt Veda shared a story about Jesus healing a blind man on the side of the road by rubbing salve on his eyes. In that moment, I experienced an immediate connection, and what I now identify as my agreement with the Divine. At five years old, I knew I was going to become a doctor. Today, I can say this matter-of-factly, but even at five years old, I knew the path was not something that was going to come easy. The first challenge that presented itself was me being born into poverty. Prior to that day, I never knew I was poor until someone told me I was. I had no idea what that even meant. I remember hearing the word "poor" and thinking it was a disease based on the way it was used toward me. When I finally understood what poverty meant, I decided I was never going to be poor again. This became my second childhood trauma.

The trauma of recognizing material poverty created a deeper wound than I could have imagined. I saw the way it materialized itself in the yin and yang of my existence, the good and the bad, and the desires that fueled my success. It led me to where I ultimately am today, but it also created an affliction to material excess.

Despite the immediate poverty, I lived a well-loved life. I enjoyed the luxury of ordinary childhood activities that included moments with family or time outdoors, and less about things that we could not afford. I had no dolls, so I made them from anything I could find. When I had no materials to create with, I spent my time daydreaming. I poured myself into dreams of things I wished to create, which eventually led to manifestations that came to life. Despite my child-like ignorance, I had no idea of the power I was exhibiting by creating with my mind.

One day, when I was about nine years old, I was outside playing by the side of the house under an apple tree when I found myself surrounded by a bright beam of light. Though it was daytime, the light appeared brighter than the Sun. Although I could not see the source of the light or anyone in particular, the light conveyed a sense of familiarity. The presence stirred a sense of love and deeper inner knowing within; this same knowing has stayed with me my entire life, and has continued to unfold over my lifetime. Though I did not have the intellectual development to understand inter-dimensional beings, this was the day I became aware of the presence of an intelligent light outside of myself.

Chapter 3:

BECOMING A DOCTOR

As I transitioned into the formal educational system, I learned and grasped the educational materials that were presented very quickly. The process came to me naturally, and I was able to comprehend and retain things with ease. But despite how much I loved listening to Aunt Veda's stories, I did not really like to read them myself. Now that I was older, she expected me to read aloud to her. Instead, I quickly figured out how to pretend I was tired so she would send me to bed early. But after a while, she caught onto my scheme and made me read regardless of how I felt; a decision I now appreciate her for.

When Aunt Veda left high-school, she became a stay-at-home mom. For a woman who was not well educated, I do not know how she knew to teach me the way she did. What may have appeared to others as an obstacle, I now know was all a part of the Divine plan.

In Jamaica, most children begin school at four years old. Aunt Veda saw something in me, and a year before I was meant to start school, she took me around to different schools and begged the teachers to give me a chance at an early start. I was accepted at just three years old, and though still suffering tremendously from separation anxiety, she would sit outside the school for hours just so I could look outside and see her there.

As I progressed through the school system, I excelled so much that the teachers allowed me to skip grades. I skipped the second and third grade, going from first all the way to the fourth grade. By the time I made it to fifth grade, I was the smallest child in the class. Despite my size in comparison to my classmates, I continued to thrive in my studies.

I was very young when I entered middle school, and this was also when my academic challenges began to present themselves. There are aspects of me that did not follow the same process as others. For one, I did not know people studied. I was very unaware that people opened a book and read it over and over to learn the material inside. As the subject matter became more complex in higher grades, I started to fall behind. I eventually got the concept of studying when I began taking chemistry, and when I did, I never looked back. Still, I did not like to read.

In adulthood, I would learn that my difficulty stemmed from undiagnosed dyslexia. In my youth, however, I coped by transferring my dislike of reading into a somewhat photographic memory. I read the pages twice and would mentally snap pictures of the information in my mind. I later accessed the information with mental recall, and was able to store it in great detail forever. It was a strategy I developed to help me avoid reading books multiple times. While it prevented me from falling behind, I did not recognize the gift that was happening, and how it would change my life.

In the 12th grade, I needed to take a standardized test, and there was after school prep work for the exam that I could not afford. After a while, school became a place for me to play with other kids. Not only did I not like to study, but I preferred to spend my time playing sports, creating arts and crafts, or being outdoors with my plants. I preferred to spend my days having a great life, playing with the other girls, and being a girly-girl. I also loved to dance and would travel around the island performing in dance and theater competitions where I won several trophies. These moments were so wonderful for me that I neglected my studies.

When the exam finally came around, I failed the national standardized test. Even when I tried to take it a year later, I failed again. Instead of going to a high-school, I was sent to a trade school.

The school system makes it fair for each student to earn their seat in high-school by passing this standardized exam. I, unfortunately, had not earned my place. Rather than head to high-school, the A team with my friends, I was sent to a secondary school, or as I called it, the B team. I was devastated.

On the island, if your family was from a certain economic class, you could buy anything or go anywhere. Living in very modest circumstances, I was not that girl. The secondary school I was forced to attend was in Montego Bay. For a while during my first year, everything was simple. I learned quickly, I always got perfect scores, I did my work, and I performed well. But it got boring very fast.

Now thirteen, I knew that this was not going to work for me. There was no way I was continuing down this road; it was not going to make me the doctor I wanted to be. One day, I walked 20 miles from where I was to a high-school called Herbert Morrison Comprehensive High School, and asked to speak with the headmaster.

I did not have an appointment, but something inside of me led me there that day. In hindsight, it was the will or maybe the angels guiding me back into the game. I knew I needed to be there. It took some time before he eventually got to me. I walked into his office, introduced myself, and explained my circumstances. I informed him that I needed to be in high-school so I could become a doctor. I knew that going to a secondary school was not going to get me there, and I needed him to give me a place in his high-school.

After listening to me intensely, and with great compassion, Mr. Lloyd Winstanley explained to me that his school was full. My heart sank. He told me to give him a week to think about it, and that I should come back then. I agreed and returned to my school. I did not tell my parents or anyone else of my plans, but for the next week, all I thought about was getting into Herbert Morrison Comprehensive High School. Each day, I would close my eyes and imagine Mr. Winstanley saying "yes" to my needs.

I also visited a catholic high-school called Mount Alvernia High School, where I spoke with the nuns. There, I told them the same story I told Mr. Winstanley about needing a place in a high-school so I could one day be a doctor. They, too, told me that their school was full, and that I needed to come back. After leaving disappointed, I waited a week before going back to see Mr. Winstanley.

The system to enter high-school was a very fair system that ensured high-school was not reserved just for the rich, but for everyone. I did not take the process seriously up until that point, but it woke me up, and forced me to stop playing; my failure was a reminder to get back in the game.

A week later, I made the 20 mile walk back to see Mr. Winstanley. The entire way here, my heart guided my little brain as I daydreamed about my own intentions. That day he finally said "yes." He notified me that I would be able to attend his high-school, and I could start the very next day. It was unbelievable. I told him that I did not have a uniform, so he offered to give me a week to come to school in whatever I wanted to wear. But within a week, he advised, my parents needed to get me a uniform. I thanked him and left.

Excitedly, I walked home, and immediately told my Aunt Veda that I would not be going back to the secondary school anymore. I was now going to be attending high-school. She could not believe it. She asked me how, and I told her everything. She was shocked that a thirteen-year-old-girl had accomplished such a task. But I had employed the force of my inner will which resulted in the manifestation of my dreams. It was something that, at the time, I had taken for granted. Now, however, I realize it was under that guidance that something had softened the headmaster's heart so he could help me carry out the Divine plan.

Getting ready for high-school was an expensive process. Buying things from uniforms to books showed me just how much of an investment school was for every parent on the island. I felt guilty that I put my Aunt Veda under such strain, but I was so relieved by the possibilities that I continued to daydream.

I revisited the headmaster one more time when I was denied the chance to study math and sciences, as it was reserved for the male students only. I went to his office and pleaded my position. As a result of my efforts, the teacher reluctantly made space for me in their classroom, and even though I did not even have a desk, I made it work. By the time I graduated high school, I had attained seven subjects in advanced level courses. It would be like graduating high-school at a level equivalent to the second year in college.

When I left high school, I realized I had no money for the next step: college. At that time, there was no formal system for student loans. Like most young teenagers, around that age, I discovered my sexuality, and shortly thereafter became pregnant. I gave birth to a baby girl who I named Rochelle, which means little rock. I was almost nineteen-years old when I became a mother. Around this time, I was also part of the organized religion known as the Seventh-day Adventist church.

While living with Aunt Veda, she was raised within the Christian faith, and by default, so was I. I became an avid churchgoer only between the ages of 15 to 18. There, I sought out new relationships and friendships, and enjoyed the fellowship the church community offered. But when I became pregnant, the church thought I committed the ultimate sin, and I was disfellowshipped, or rejected, if you will. In the eyes of organized religion, being pregnant and unwed is a sin. The church's policy is to publicly accept your sin, and be re-baptized in order to be reaccepted into the fold of the church. I thought the rule was cruel. I was never going to prostrate myself in order to be accepted by anyone, so I chose to bring forth my child.

Rochelle grew up to become a creator in her own right, and has remained another cornerstone of my life. My childhood traumas of abandonment, followed by rejection at the hands of organized religion, were pivotal points in my life that forced changes on my path for which I am eternally grateful. Rejection by the Christian church forced me to seek God in other places. In turn, I explored other religions, and it was then that I discovered Buddhism. Through this practice, I was introduced to meditation at a very early age.

The church that I had loved, grown up within, served, and was a role model to many of the young kids and young adults, turned its back on me. It was my first encounter with the dark night of the Soul; a period in which I encountered challenges and growth, and my intuition, along with the "knowing," became the only footprints in the sands of my life.

Somehow, after that initial disappointment, and during this dark night, I became comfortable in my own company and being. It was also during solitude that I discovered what I now refer to as the "knowing;" a deep sense of a presence—someone or something—that is always with me on my left side. During this time, my intuition expanded and I was learning from it.

I experienced a great pain when I became separated from my church friends, and the boy for whom I became pregnant. The father of my unborn child was only a year older than I was, and had already moved on to another woman. This caused me immense feelings of jealousy and rejection. From that moment, I vowed to never experience pain like that again. I began to learn how to let go.

Letting go was how I surmounted my first childhood trauma of separation anxiety. I learned to let go of people and things that provided external comfort, and began to cling to the inner comfort that was now surrounding me and the child I was nurturing inside me. Through these uncomfortable life changing experiences, I learned very early on how to hold things lightly in the palm of my hands. It was the best way to keep things, family, and even friends the longest. Whenever I held on too tightly, they seemed to disappear from my life as if holding grains of sand in my hand; the tighter I squeezed, the more they fell through the cracks of my fingers.

In an attempt to protect myself from further pain, and at the tender age of twenty, I adopted a new concept for my life that mirrored that of a rocket. When a rocket ascends, it first drops the fuselage, followed by all its remaining parts. In the end, all that is left behind is the cockpit, its smallest and loneliest part. If I was going to ascend, everyone and everything in my life would need to be released.

I grew to understand how to release the things that no longer served me. Adopting this concept early in my life allowed me to spend more alone time in meditation. In these moments of silence, I developed a greater curiosity about the Universe.

Upon becoming a mother, I entered the workforce. This was when I met Richard, the love of my life, and the man who I would marry about 10 years later. For the first year of my daughter's life, I worked full time to save money, and with plans to attend college. During this time, I loved and educated my beautiful Rochelle. As I adjusted to motherhood, the "knowing" within me told me I needed to be in the United States. Most of my cousins and extended family lived in England, so my Aunt Veda thought it would be the natural thing to do. But I had zero interest in going to England. I was determined to be in America. My heart was set on it, and, subconsciously, I understood this was a part of a greater plan.

My journey to becoming a doctor was beginning to look like it was not going to be realized. I needed a secondary education, and I knew I needed to be in the United States to make this happen.

I applied and received an offer of acceptance from Columbia University with a partial scholarship. However, in order to get a student visa, I needed participation from my father, or sperm donor, who was now a singer in New York City. He failed to complete and return the forms that were sent to him, and just like that, that door to my dream was closed.

While disappointed, I was not going to let that stop me. Instead, I decided to try again. In the meantime, I went to college in Kingston, Jamaica. After college, and in my early twenties, I worked in a laboratory as a certified medical laboratory technologist doing analytical testing in microbiology, clinical chemistry, and hematology. But in my heart, I knew I still needed to get to America.

I eventually applied to Howard University and was accepted, but without a scholarship. Despite this, I somehow knew this was where I needed to be. It felt right. It took a village, but I was able to receive a lot of assistance from several people. Due to this, I eventually raised enough money to get a student visa to the United States. As part of the process, I had to demonstrate, via bank statements, that I had enough money to pay for my college and living expenses for the first year.

When I started college at Howard University, I quickly realized that the coursework contained material I already knew from my Jamaican high-school and college experiences. Although this should have been a sense of relief, I, instead, felt a sense of terror. I had a fixed budget, and a specific amount of money that needed to last me for a year. I could not spend it idly.

I spoke to the college counselor who advised me to contact the Dean of Arts and Science. I met with the Dean where I presented my concerns. After much consideration, she made an offer. She advised me that I could test out the classes, if I wanted to. She offered me a chance to come back the following Friday to sit examinations for the classes I proposed I test out. I was so excited for the opportunity. I did not know what to expect since I had never taken an exam in the United States before, but I told her that I would be there. The next week, I sat exams for the entire first year of college—math, chemistry, organic chemistry, and physics—all in one day.

Once I received my results, I was able to start my second year of college, though it was a similar experience to the first. After sitting in on a few classes, I was once again disappointed. I went back to the Dean and petitioned to test out, and she obliged. Within days of arriving in the United States, I was starting college at a third-year level. In just under two weeks, I had tested out of the first- and second-year college-level courses in mathematics, science, organic chemistry, general chemistry, English, and physics. With focus and determination, and multiple-choice after multiple-choice tests, it was successfully over. I was in a new country, and was, again, exercising the will.

Now, in my third year, I began doing medical laboratory technology because I knew that it would be the easiest way for me to do something I was familiar with.

I was able to start working as a phlebotomist. Every morning, I would go into the hospital at 4 a.m., draw blood from patients, and then attend my classes. While most students took 15 credits per semester, at the suggestion of a guidance counselor, I did the same. But then I realized it was just not enough. I was bored to tears. I went back to the Dean and explained to her that I was paying in cash for my education. I wanted to know whether taking additional credits would cost me more money, and to my surprise, she said "no." I immediately added 15 more credits for a total of 30 credits per semester. In addition to my credit load, I also maintained my job at the hospital. I barely slept, but I studied hard. I was so motivated to get my family out of poverty that I knew exactly what I had to do.

When my first year was over, I was broke and had no idea how I was going to pay for the final year. I was an international student, so although I was smart, I did not qualify for most of the available scholarships at that time. The student counselor guided me to apply for a scholarship from the World Health Organization. There were only five slots available, and of the thousands of international students in the United States, I was one of the chosen five. Twenty thousand dollars later, my second year of college was paid for.

With my eyes set on my Divine plan to be a doctor, I continued to work hard. By the end of my second year, I finished my four-year degree.

I graduated summa cum laude. With great gratitude, I wrote a poem that was chosen to be printed on all of the graduation invitations for the College of Arts and Science commencement ceremony in 1996. After graduation, I left Washington D.C. and headed to Fort Myers, Florida to be with the love of my life, Richard Moulton. By now, I was beginning to see a clear pattern in the dance of the Universe, and the dedication of the village it took to get me here.

Richard, Rochelle, and I settled in as a family in our little apartment on Crystal Drive, and I took a job at Naples Hospital in the laboratory where I was once again able to work and save. During this time, Richard was doing his MBA at the University of South Florida, and got me interested in the stock market. Following in his footsteps, that interest turned to an obsession. I was still too broke to go anywhere or to take on any more classes, so I drove to Barnes and Noble and, with the little money I was earning, I read every book I could find on the stock market.

With a new boost of confidence, I went for it. I picked a few good stocks, studied the papers, debated and disagreed with Richard about his choices, and that was how I eventually landed Walmart stock. When its split multiplied, I got close to fifty thousand to pay for my first year of medical school. Since then, I have taught myself a lot more about the stock market, and intuition has always watched from my shoulders.

Twelve months later, when I finally applied to medical school, I was accepted at George Washington University in D.C., and Meharry Medical College in Tennessee. It was not difficult to choose between the two. Meharry reminded me of the love I felt on the campus at Howard University, so I went to Meharry Medical College. As a junior student, I became part of Alpha Omega Alpha, which is an Honor Society for the top one percent of doctors in the United States. I was in that one percent, and because of this, I could choose any place I wanted to attend for residency when I graduated.

When I entered medical school, my agreement with the Divine was to do internal medicine, which I knew to be the type of medicine that made a difference in human life. Somewhere along the line, my ego got the best of me. It told me that I was exceptionally brilliant, and that money was more important than anything else. I still had the photographic memory of an elephant, and, because of this, everything continued to come easily to me. I understood the game, and knew that if you were really smart, you could go anywhere. I made 95 percent on the first test I took, followed by 98 percent on my second test. Apparently, my performance was so out of this world that I got lost in the shuffle.

I was at Vanderbilt University doing surgery on rotation when I somehow ended up working on a case for a bilateral cochlear implant; a first of its kind in the United States. The surgeon I worked with was so wonderful and gentle with the patient. When we put in the cochlear implant, the patient was suddenly able to hear. I was mesmerized by it all, and thought to myself, "Wow, this is what I want to do." In the stories of the Bible that Aunt Veda read to me as a child, it depicted Jesus healing a man's eyes. Well, I was going to heal the ears of the masses.

I learned surgeons made a lot more money than internists. Before I knew it, I got sidetracked, and was neglecting my purpose for going into medicine. I initially wanted to become a head and neck surgeon, and that year I was flown around the country by different colleges. I visited so many residency programs that wanted me, but I chose to go to the Mayo Clinic. That was a massive accomplishment to me.

As a surgeon, I quickly began to lose myself in my work and my ego. I fell deep into materialism, and the grind took over my life. The more I worked, the more I began to feel an internal discordance. Though I was on top of my game, even writing research papers that I was lucky enough to travel around the country to present on behalf of the Mayo Clinic's ENT department, in the midst of it all, I realized I made a mistake.

As I worked for more money, I was also raising my daughter, Rochelle, who was now thirteen, to drive. I knew it was illegal, but I needed her to transport me to the hospital, but also drive herself to school. With my husband employed in Fort Myers, I was only able to see him every four months while I was in training. "What am I doing?", I asked myself. I realized I was not playing my part in the greater plan. Even as I trained, I was choosing the possibility of the income I could earn in the future over the people I loved most—Richard and Rochelle. After two and a half years, I chose my family. I changed my specialty to internal medicine at the University of Miami, in Miami, Florida. Within two years, I was able to complete my medical training and return to Fort Myers to practice, but best of all, to be closer to Richard.

In Fort Myers, I was employed by a hospital system. The culture was different from every other medical system I was engaged with, and the "knowing" knew it was not the place for me. It was not Meharry Medical College, it was not Vanderbilt University, it was not the Mayo Clinic, either. I knew I could not stay there, and after five years of working in internal medicine in the hospital system, I left to start my own company.

I named my clinic the Listening Doctor, due to divine intervention. I came up with the name because patients always wrote notes on my evaluation saying how well I listened. This name also embodied my personal belief that patients live in their own bodies, and understood it best. I also recognized that when patients spoke, if I listened long enough, I could hear the things in between the lines that they felt, but did not say.

My patients would tell me the entire story, while giving me the subjective and objective details I needed for a true diagnosis and better treatment plan. Subconsciously, I had no idea what the true meaning of the name "the Listening Doctor" really meant, but in time, it eventually revealed itself.

Chapter 4:

INTUITION RISING

When I settled into my role in service to humanity as "the Listening Doctor," unaware to me, my service as a doctor was also a service to myself. While my profession served as a mirror through which I viewed the world, it was also the platform upon which my illusions of reality were shattered.

The events surrounding the progression of my natural psionic abilities as a fundamental part of my humanness, is what I describe as "mysticism rising." I am no novice to life events happening at the right time, the proverbial thinking of someone as they randomly call, or even having a dream that manifests in life, frame for frame. I am sure we have all shared similar events. I now realize that they were serving as reminders and check points in a system beyond the illusion of life that I did not know exists.

One day, I was taking the history of a new patient to my practice. He was a young man, about 28 years old. While typing his information into the computer, I perceived him telling me that his mother died from breast cancer, and felt the deep sense of grief he was experiencing. So, with compassion, I turned to him and said,

"Yes, tell me about that."

"Tell you about what?" he asked me.

I looked at him perplexed, but calmly responded, "Your mother's passing from breast cancer."

Shocked, he replied, "How do you know that?"

Stunned by this response, I looked at him and asked, "How do I know what?"

"About my mother's breast cancer."

"You just told me," I replied to the young man who was now looking at me in a very quizzical way.

"I did not say anything to you about her breast cancer," he said to me firmly.

"Yes, you did. You just told me."

After much back and forth, I paused in the hopes of moving on with his visit. But inside, I was very certain I had heard him loud and clear, in the same cadence, voice, and tone in which he spoke.

Reality was, he truly had not spoken. I must admit, this was not the first time that something like this happened between my patients and myself. But something about this encounter forced me into accepting that something was off.

These events were happening for many years prior, but I had always passed them off as coincidence. I vividly remember my encounter with a patient I will call Elizabeth. I was very excited to see her, because I wanted to ask her about her recent vacation to Mexico with her sister. As soon as she got settled into her visit, and I began taking her blood pressure, I excitedly said to her,

"Tell me about your visit to Mexico with your sister!"

She paused, looked up at me, and said, "What are you talking about?"

With the same level of excitement, I repeated the question,

"Your trip to Mexico!"

This time she said, "I didn't tell you about that trip."

I completed her vitals, sat to face her, and reminded her that she did indeed tell me.

She proceeded,

"There is no way I would have told you. The last time I saw you was in January, and it was not until May that I decided to plan the trip with my sister. I only went to Mexico two weeks ago, and I just got back, so there's no way I could have told you."

Despite what she had just shared, I was convinced she told me. I knew she did, and after trying to convince her, I eventually gave up.

But after many years of these occurrences, and now the young man, I began a process of introspection. I realized that I was experiencing something I lived with my whole life; some kind of telepathic mind reading. I also realized that, when in sync with a patient, unstressed, unnerved, and focused, I sometimes answered the patient's question before they voiced words.

This repeated practice got me into a pickle with patients because, from time to time, they were upset that I was not allowing them to speak. But, to me, they had already spoken and I had heard it. In their voice, in their tone, and delivered with the same emotions they were feeling.

Frankly, I was oblivious that I was reading their mind. I guess because I was operating from a place of intuition all my life, it did not occur to me that this was not something everyone experienced.

I failed to recognize my high sense of intuition as the under-discussed part of my being. Because it was so integrated into my daily practice, it was a silly assumption to believe everyone operated from this place of "knowing." This high sense of intuition allowed me to serve my patients well and with distinction. It was not what they said that I heard, it was what they thought.

This information allowed me to kindly and gently intrude, as I brought forth my perspective and advice. This was not always well received by my patients, family, or friends, for that matter. But over the years, I learned how to hone the skill, and, at times, suppress it.

Intuition is not something that can actually be suppressed. I discovered that it was a true part of being human, and, like any skill, it grows and matures with time. It was the same intuition that whispered in my ears, telling me to examine a patient's abdomen in order to discover something lurking that they are unaware of. It also inspired me to order tests that would eventually unveil pathology leading treatment that prolonged a patient's life.

Saying this out loud, one would think that one or all of these mind reading encounters would cause a person like me to slow down and become introspective sooner. But, I did not. I barrelled right on through it in ignorance. I was not appreciating this as anything different or special, but after my encounter with the young man, his reaction held a mirror to my face, and forced me to ask, "What is going on?"

In the quest for answers, I came up with a strategy. Whenever I got a strong intuition from a patient, I kindly started by saying, "I'm going to ask you something. Please do not be offended, but let me know if I am right or wrong." I then proceeded to share with the patient what I was sensing or feeling, and what I heard telepathically. In each case, they admitted that I was right. After the affirmation, I verified that they never shared the information with me.

I gradually learned to decipher when I was receiving telepathic information, and when I actually heard the patient's spoken voice. Initially, to me, they were one and the same. But with time, I was able to clearly separate the two. What I discovered about myself during those times was that my heart served as a receiver for telepathy, and my brain was the receiver for the spoken word.

My cardiac receiver resides in an area or a triangular field of energy between the level of my heart, and runs all the way up to my ear. One vertex of the triangle points to the base of my neck ending at my brainstem, while the other two points correspond with my shoulders to complete the triangle in my upper torso. It was that very intense energy field that I felt being activated during times when my intuition received information via telepathic encounters.

As a medical doctor, I have no scientific explanation for these experiences, and cannot say anyone taught them to me. But I have lived them, so I am sharing them with you. Over my lifetime, I heard stories and comments about intuition so I resorted to accepting this sense and activated energy as my intuition. These psionic episodes manifested in ways that were so subtle, and often seamless in my daily life.

Walk with me through a few of these varied mystical, yet very human experiences.

I was about five years old when I first encountered what I called "shadow people." These are beings who are very tall, about 6 to 7 feet tall, with exceptionally long limbs. They appeared as a dark translucent hologram that only I could perceive. The hologram has no facial features, but no well-defined gender I deduced from the appearance. They seem to live and operate among us in a dimension that exists parallel to our earthly dimension. I was never afraid, as my encounters with these beings were brief and almost fleeting. They never seemed to be aware of my presence.

In Jamaican culture, this occurrence is so commonplace that it is referred to as seeing a "duppy," or a ghost. I grew up hearing stories of ghostly experiences all my life from family, neighbors, and even members of the church. It was not something I sought to experience, and it was neither encouraged or praised.

One of my earliest encounters with the shadow beings was at the end of one of my school days. I could not wait to get home from school to see Aunt Veda. One evening, when I entered the house, I heard something moving in the kitchen. I headed towards the kitchen to greet her, but when I got there, I saw a vague, dark, defined shadow of a person's hand retracting through the window. I thought Aunt Veda was outside taking something through the window, so without thinking, I headed outside. When I got outside to the side of the kitchen, there was no one there.

These holographic shadows move quickly, while other times, their hologram appears sustained. Let me explain. One day I was walking down the street with a friend and could see a lady coming towards us. My friend,

Nicole, and I were engaged in a conversation, walking closely beside each other. As the lady approached us, she walked in a straight line, passing between my friend and I. What got my attention when she traversed us was that she did not deviate from her path. It forced me to move out the way ever so slightly to give her room to transit her path. As the lady passed us, she smelled of an awful odor. I commented on her body odor to my friend saying, "My goodness, that lady smells so awful, and she almost mowed me over." My friend turned back to look in the direction I mentioned, then looked at me oddly, replying,

"What lady?"

I replied, "The one that just walked by us." But when we both turned around, there was no one there. For as far back as we could both see, there was no one there. It would have taken the woman at least five minutes on her walk to approach me, so even if my mind thought it had seen something, it would be a sustained visual image of a person in my dimension. This was also one of the few times that the shadow was less holographic, and seemed composed of more of physical substance.

It was because of this cultural acceptance that, as a child, I resorted to accepting the status quo. So, when on occasions I was visited by inter-dimensional beings, I never discussed it with any adults. I just resorted to the understanding that these were ghosts.

One of my most profound inter-dimensional experiences was an encounter with my maternal grandparents when I was nine-years-old. Prior to that, I never had the grace of meeting my mother's parents, Jane and Joshua Smith; they died before I was born. To this day, this episode remains vivid in my mind.

While playing in my mother's yard with my younger brother, Donovan—the first of two sons she gave birth to when she returned to her husband—three people appeared at the fence. They were all well-dressed in suits. There was a lady of short stature with very long hair who was accompanied by a gentleman standing to her left. He was taller than her, stout, and with greying hair. Behind them stood a third man who was much taller than the other two, and stood there in silence.

The shorter of the two men asked me for my mother, Elsa. I told him she was not at home. He asked me if I knew who he was, and I said "no." He told me he was Elsa's father, and my grandfather. He told me to tell her that he could not wait, and that his house was getting wet whenever it rained.

Clearly, I was very aware that my grandparents were dead, but in this scenario, they were very much alive, and as interactive as I was. I relayed the message to my mother, and my Aunt Veda. As I described the people in great detail, I discovered that the clothes they appeared in were actually the outfits they had been buried in. I would have had no way of knowing that as they had died at least 30 years before I was born, and there were no pictures of them that I had ever seen.

Two weeks after my ancestral encounter, my aunt and the rest of my family packed up the family car and we drove from Montego Bay to Saint Elizabeth to visit my grandfather's grave site. When we arrived, we realized that he was buried close to a tree whose roots had cracked the top of his tombstone, which had now caved in. It seemed that this was the message he wished to relay to my mother. He was given a new cover for his tomb.

There is some cognitive discordance in the human mind between the apparent dead and the living. The belief that when a person exits the body they cease to exist is this a backward belief system that is preventing us from advancing our species, and enhancing our psionic natural telepathic abilities. I cannot explain how my dead brother-in-law, George, gave me a message to relay to his wife, Maxine, that contained private details I had no way of knowing. Or how my dead childhood neighbour gave me a message to give her daughter I had not seen in over ten years. She wanted her to know that her granddaughter was pregnant. At times, some messages seem trivial, but they hold great significance in the lives of the receiver. Over the years, I never gave much significance to this kind of communication, nor do I seek them or encourage them; they just happen.

An out of body experience, or OBE for short, is another form of inter-dimensional interaction, but one in which the very fabric of spacetime changes. My first childhood out of body experience occurred around the age of twelve. I found myself in what appeared to be a dream, standing at the foot of the bed of a woman I hardly knew. She was a friend of my mother named Ms. Ivy who resided about 10 miles away from my house. She was not in pain, but appeared to be sleeping. She was tucked in a sheet with her big toe exposed. I noticed as her toe spasmed and in that instant, I knew she was dead. Around me were other people asking who she was, but it was me who identified her, calling her by her name, Ms. Ivy.

The next morning, I told my aunt that a friend of my mother had died last night. She asked me how I knew this, and I told her that I had seen the lady dying in my dream. About four hours later, my mother showed up to share the news that her friend had died.

At that moment, I passed it off as nothing more than a dream. Though it was so real, as a child, I had no way of communicating the experience to those around me other than to say it was a dream. By calling it that, it became something everyone understood, and could relate to. But to me, I knew it was real.

I continued to have dreams and premonitions throughout my life. It was the visions in dreams that forced me to shut down these experiences. I would have clear dreams of future events, some of which were catastrophic, and it bothered me to no end. I saw an accident involving my brother two weeks before it occurred. That day, I begged him to stay home, and he did. But two weeks later, when I let my guards down, it manifested, and he landed in the emergency room due to a motor vehicle accident. I felt as though it should have been something I could have prevented. What good was it to see the future if no one benefited from my knowledge? After numerous dreams and corresponding manifested events, I prayed for it to all go away, and for a few years, it abated. In my later years when it finally returned, it was much stronger and impossible to ignore.

This same "knowing" presence that has always been with me often knocked and prodded at me; an invasion that occurred until it acted through me.

There was a patient who I will refer to as Gidget, and who I found myself thinking of for an entire week. I had a recurrent nudge to call her, but I kept ignoring the prod. She was not sick, and so, I had no real reason to call her. But she stayed on my mind. One afternoon, while I was in the office, my intuition to call her was so strong, it overtook me. It told me I had to call her right away because she needed me. I sat down at my desk, picked up the phone, and dialed. When she answered the phone, she was crying.

"Have you heard?" she asked.

"Heard what?" I responded.

Her husband had just fallen dead on the floor. I was in disbelief. She proceeded to tell me that her husband just died just a few minutes before my call. His body was barely cold, and the EMTs were currently there trying to revive him. Somehow, I knew she needed me.

It got me thinking about when I had a strong premonition that Richard, my husband, was going to have a bicycle accident. Unbeknownst to him, I drove along Summerlin Road for a week at 5 a.m., in the darkness of each morning, to ensure he was okay. One morning, I saw him riding along Summerlin Road so I drove up beside him to say hello. He was surprised and annoyed that I was up so early, driving around for what appeared to be no clear reason. A week later, on July 4th, 2019, he was knocked off his bicycle on the Sanibel Bridge, shattering his wrist and hip. Immediately after the accident, his phone miraculously called me. I answered on the first ring, but no one responded. It was just an open line. I listened in terror to the silence that was followed by the bustling and distant voices of bystanders who attempted to help him. I shouted his name into the open phone line, but no one answered. I eventually hung up and sat there in anticipation. He eventually called me to tell me he was in an accident. I felt it coming, I saw it, even, and went looking for it weeks before it happened.

After this, and a series of other events, it got me thinking. What was happening was not normal. There had to be something wrong with me. Yet, when I thought about all the synchronicities that were taking place, like me thinking of a person and them immediately calling or texting, they could not all be coincidences.

The events also got me thinking about other instances where I would walk into a room where there was the presence of an energy that I could not see. It would cause all the hairs in the psionic receiver located at the back of my neck to stand on edge. It also got me thinking about a time when I was in a hotel room with Richard preparing for a bicycle ride. He wanted the blinds down for privacy, and I wanted them up for sunlight. Just before I went to sleep, I manually put them down. However, when I woke up, I looked at them just as we both witnessed the manual blinds slam shut on their own. At that moment, we agreed that what had taken place was not normal. But that was only one of the many inadvertent abilities to affect physical matter around me. I still am not clear how it works.

These life experiences, and my intuition intensified to a place where I could no longer ignore them. I was now in my early forties, and right before my eyes was the occasional encounter with what appeared to be flashes of light. I later discovered that these were orbs of light. These lights can be captured on film, and as time unfolded, I discovered that they were actual living conscious energy beings that appear to be made of plasma. They would later play an integral part in my own discovery.

I was in my mid-forties when I observed that I was able to communicate with some animals, snakes in particular. I began to notice these odd "coincidences" unfolding all around me. Every time I saw a snake, it would be followed by a strange life changing event, good or bad. I would have snake encounters in my dreams, and very clear messages were delivered that later manifested in this lifetime. I would also have real life encounters, as simple as running into a snake in the yard, and the same pattern of good or bad messages would be delivered. The messages were always clear and delivered to me in a telepathic way.

There were a few people in my life that I felt comfortable sharing these experiences with: my husband, Richard, my daughter, Rochelle, and my friends, Lisa and Laura. Whenever I saw a snake, I would call Laura to tell her the message I got and waited. Each time, in less than two weeks, the message would manifest. I now better understand the law of attraction, so if I am creating these events, I can tell you that I am very good at it. But I prefer to just accept it as a dance with the Universe.

I now understand that if and when I dream or encounter a snake, it is a message usually directed at me. They always seem to appear when I have pending turmoil or a revelation, and act as a forerunner in emotionally preparing me for what was about to unfold.

One day, I left work to head home for lunch and ran into a snake. I immediately called Laura to tell her the message I received. I knew that I was going to lose an employee. It was Brittany. After lunch, I walked into the office, called a meeting and asked, "who is leaving?" Everyone was shocked that I knew, and fell silent. I watched on as they all looked at each other from the corner of their eyes, accusing each other of telling me.

I am certain that not everyone has intuitive experiences to the extreme that I have. But the truth is, we all do experience them. I am sure you can relate to feeling like you have antennas around your ears at times. If I am in the room or in traffic, and someone is staring at me, I can instantly feel the person looking at me. The strange thing is, I would turn around and look directly at the person, holding their gaze. When out and about or at a function, I did not need to look around the room to see who was looking at me as I would instinctively look directly at the person who was staring at me. Our eyes would connect, and we would hold each other's gaze until one of us eventually gave out. I joke with friends to never stare at me because I can feel it.

As I am sharing this book with you, I can say I finally came full circle into fully accepting my rising mysticism. The gifts that I ran away from all my life were now more palatable to me as I became more scientifically curious. The frequent mind reading encounters started to wake me up to reality that there was a whole lot more to life than what meets the eye. I was now accepting that the fabric of the world is interactive.

As we all know, what we see as an increased intuitive self-awareness, and in the path of spiritual growth, nothing moves in a straight line. There are turns and corners along a very timely road. However, during this time, my brain told me it was all a matter of rational reasoning for the events that were meant to unfold. The ego, the auto-processing of the brain, was in charge while the Soul, the intuitive part of the human, patiently observed.

The experiences I described are in no way unique to me, and I am certain we have all experienced them at some time or another. I utilized the energy of the "knowing" to guide my work with patients, but I executed the guidance with such ingratitude due to not "seeing" or appreciating the gift at the time. I was lost in my ego and somewhat blinded by my drive to succeed. I was falling deep into a life of materialism, and buried in shallow friendships and frivolous activities. I was unknowingly lost, but from the outside, I was the very definition of what success looked like for many. The truth is, I was in discordance with my life's purpose; a plan that I was unknowingly a part of.

When I forced myself to stop and be more introspective, my life began to turn; the sine wave, the mandala had completed its circle, and the game of life took on a new intensity. Whether I was ready or not, my Soul and intuition were about to grow in ways I could never have imagined.

Chapter 5:

STRENGTH VIA THE PATH OF SURRENDER

March, 2020, changed the life of all of humanity. My last beautiful memory before the change was a vacation to Cuba where I traveled with some friends. Immediately upon my return, I was attending the book signing for my daughter's first book in Barnes and Noble when the United States went into lockdown. It was the beginning of the event that would later be known as the COVID-19 pandemic.

During the pandemic, I made a promise to the Universe and to myself, that I was not going to be one of those doctors who hid behind a mask. I refused to serve out of fear for my own life. I was ready and willing to sacrifice my life to serve humanity. The intensity of the chaos surrounding the pandemic took precedence, and scientific curiosity for my own psionics lost importance. After the COVID-19 pandemic, life as we knew it changed. The isolation we all experienced forced a contraction of my world, and during that time, I made a seamless transition to focus on my family.

Two years after the lockdown, the world was normalizing. Like most people, I was ready to re-enter the changed world. I was most excited to resume my life, especially my annual vacations with my daughter, Rochelle, and my grandchildren, Landon who was 10, and Serenity, who had just turned 2 years old. I was looking forward to returning to what I considered to be myself, and the identity I had adopted as my life.

But soon after, Hurricane Ian touched down in Florida on September 28, 2022, changing my life, and shattering the glass of illusion surrounding me forever.

I am often hesitant to talk about this turning point in my life, as it is a pivotal point in my spiritual journey. As humans, we seem to identify major changes with trauma, and this is true for sure. Maybe the hurricane, in some ways, was traumatic for me, but trauma varies in the eyes of the beholder. I grew up on an island where there is great respect for the power of the wind, but there is no fear of the display of its power. So, despite the events of that day, like any other hurricane, I was mesmerized by the power of the wind, and experienced no fear.

In the early morning of the day Hurricane Ian landed, around 4 a.m., my intuition, "the knowing," woke me up. I acknowledged the "knowing," a strong presence around me, and headed downstairs. As I opened the sliding glass doors to my patio, the air was quiet, and the wind chimes were sounding in the gentle wind. It was dark, but I could sense a strong intense energy in my backyard. The flashes of light I appreciated as orbs were everywhere.

I immediately took out my cell phone to record the light rain and force of the wind, and that was when I saw them on camera. I saw several plasma orbs of light everywhere. I felt a sense of peace and calm radiating from them as they darted quickly in every direction while creating a vibrant glow due to the sheer number of them. I have seen orbs in all different places, and in varying circumstances. I have seen single orbs, and even multiple orbs, but in this encounter, they were large and more abundant.

I have also come to understand that people have encountered orbs of light under many documented circumstances. What I can say is, not only do they appear in the distant sky, but I also experience them in my immediate surroundings. From observation, the orbs in the sky are large, sometimes massive and visible to my naked eyes. The orbs in my immediate surroundings are not always visible to the naked eye, but they can be captured on camera. When I observe them during daytime hours, they appear as flashes of light. I see them so frequently that my experience with them became normalized.

On this particular day, I interpreted my encounter with the orbs and the sense of safety I felt amongst them to mean the hurricane was coming, and I was going to be safe. It was that sense of safety that I felt and communicated to friends who advised me to evacuate, which I refused to do. My intention was to have a glass of wine and charcuterie, and experience the power of wind.

By 8 a.m. that morning, the winds began to pick up. As the hurricane approached us and the winds intensified, I felt so secure that I tried to go to sleep in the middle of the hurricane. My husband, Richard, who is a part of the emergency rescue committee (EOC) for the City of Fort

Myers, called me with panic in his voice. He wanted me to check if the water in the preserve in our backyard was flooding. The preserve is a large area of landmass that serves as a catchment area for rising ocean water. It absorbs ocean water at high tide, and in doing so, it mitigates flooding. A large portion of this landmass is in my backyard.

I heard the emotions in my husband's voice as he explained that the city had just registered a very high tidal wave warning for the beach. He explained that the wave was so high, their monitoring device could not register a reading. This meant that a tidal wall well over 15 feet of water was heading my way.

Reluctantly, I looked outside through the bedroom window and saw that the water in the preserve was rising. The water was higher than usual, but areas that were normally dry were now covered with water. I was fascinated that the water was clear and pristine, and I watched in awe as the water rose from the preserve, onto the grass in my backyard. At that point, I decided to go back outside to capture pictures of the water and the wind. I was taking pictures outside when I heard a loud banging inside my house. I thought, "What in the world?" as I walked back toward the sound.

The sound was coming from the front of the house. As I approached the front door, I peered through the glass door to see water gushing down the street. The waters were high, murky, and loud, as the roaring ocean had come into my community. I watched as cars floated down the street, as furniture and debris moved right along with them. The six-foot-high mailboxes were lost under the height of the water. Within five minutes of Richard's call we were flooded.

I wanted to capture the scene, so I went upstairs to the window to get a better view. There was noise everywhere created by the wind, rain, and flood waters. Despite the noise, I could hear a very distinct banging sound. I was certain that this sound was coming from inside the house. I started toward the direction of the sound and realized it was coming from inside the garage. I went around the corner, down the hallway, and toward the door that led to the garage.

I opened the door, and by reflex, I shut it instantly. I slammed the door, and stood there for at least 10 seconds. I remember pressing my fingers against my eyes as if to unsee what I had just seen. I had never, ever, in all my life experienced that feeling. I felt defeated. I was finally aware that the water was about to enter my house; it was stronger than I, and there was nothing I could do about it. For the first time in my life, I surrendered.

I opened the door again to see that the water was still there. I had to face it. I looked around in the garage, and could see the deep freezer and garbage pan floating about. Boxes were tilted everywhere. My husband's red Nismo sports car was filled with water, and the car horn was squealing. The water in the street continued to push against the metal garage door banging to come in, while the water already inside the garage worked its way up the steps.

I thought this water was going to come in, and that maybe I should move some stuff from downstairs to the first floor. My furniture was so incredibly oversized that it would have been futile trying to lift anything on my own to move them out of the way of the incoming floodwaters.

As I surrendered, every muscle in my body relaxed, and my shoulders slumped, submitting to the spirit of the water. In an instant, I

47

gave up the fight against the flood waters. I decided to lay on my bed and wait. I had no more moves. I waited for the Universe to make her next move. About 20 minutes later, I was now in full acceptance of the current situation, anticipating at least a foot of water in the house. I slowly got up to look over the balcony to the downstairs floor, expecting to see flood waters inside the house. But there was no water on the floor. I was perplexed.

I descended the stairs and proceeded toward the garage entry door. When I opened it, the water had receded by one foot. I fell to the floor on my knees in gratitude, and thanked the Universe. I wanted to cry, but I could not make the tears.

The natural activity of the tide started pulling the water back from land, and into the ocean. I was at my breaking point, and I could not handle any more challenges. I had dedicated the last two years of my life to others in the name of COVID, and it left me emotionally exhausted. COVID was such a monumental event in all our lives, but for me, it was not personal. Humanity was under attack, and I was there to be of tireless service.

But this hurricane and flooding felt personal. The waters had come for me. Everything in my life had happened through water. I descended to Earth as a spirit from my mother's womb into water, I was birthed through and from that water, 80 percent of my body is made up of water. And when I die, I will go back to these same waters. It is all about water.

The part of Mother Earth that stored memories had finally returned to remind me of Her great work. I wanted to undo all the damage that this water, this blessed water, had brought into my garage. I was still blinded to the fact that this blessed water, disguised as a flood and cloaked in mud, was coming to cleanse me. It was reaching out to me to say, "wake up, wake up!", and I was finally beginning to hear the whisper.

I was facing the flood waters as the wind continued to howl outside. Eventually, I lost electricity and all phone communications. My friend, Margie, who, via phone, was serving as my eyes, and was updating me on the news could no longer reach me. My community was an ocean, isolated in darkness. I thought about the sense of safety I felt in the presence of the orbs, and though emotionally broken, my body was safe. Although my garage was flooded, the house was standing. I was grateful.

In the thick darkness, I climbed the stairs, one foot at a time, in exhaustion. I laid my body back onto the bed and passed out.

I woke up around 5:30 a.m. the next morning and the wind had dissipated. It was dawn, it was quiet, and the air was still. I looked through the window, and I could see from upstairs that the water was still in the streets. The gushing waters from a few hours ago were now settled at least three feet high in the street. Fishes were swimming around with tadpoles making little circles in the shallow parts.

I opened the front door and inhaled the fresh still air. The atmosphere was cool. It is something that happens after a hurricane—a sense that the world loves you and all is beautiful, as if it had not just tried to kill you; a living demonstration of the irony of entropy and order. It was a reminder that, after all, you must destroy to create. Symbolically, I was destroyed, and, therefore, my creation had just begun.

As the day broke, my neighbors gathered on the sidewalk and realized the level of catastrophe. I sprang into action checking on my neighbors, and once everyone was accounted for, I began planning my next steps. It never dawned on me that this destruction was not caused by rain water. I thought that the damage from the water in the garage would be easy to clean up as it was just rain, but I was wrong. I was not prepared for the level of destruction that the salt water delivered; it killed everything it touched. Everything corroded overnight. What remained was a heavy layer of silt, a level of thin soil and muck, everywhere in its path. The indescribable odor of a flood is unforgettable.

The neighborhood was surrounded by water, and was only accessible by boat. Families were isolated, and my neighborhood was inaccessible to the outside world for three days. It was on that third day when one of my employees came into the neighborhood through the wading water to check on me. She brought trail nuts, which I love. Up until that point, I did not realize that I had not put a single piece of food in my mouth for over seventy-two hours. We lost electrical power, and had lost all the food I planned on eating post-hurricane. It was in the fridge in the garage that was floating in muck. I was in survival mode.

Rochelle, my grandchildren, and my husband, Richard, were also unable to come into the community until the water receded, which took three days. I could see the tears in Richard's eyes. I felt his pain as our catastrophic loss sank in. He felt a sense of guilt for leaving me home alone, but I knew his commitment and service to this city was of priority. And I knew I could take care of myself.

For the first time in a long time, I saw him cry. It was Richard who then delivered to me the extent of the disaster. Rochelle was at a loss for words, but it was my granddaughter who emphatically felt me the most. She kept telling me that my house was broken, and gave me the most loving hugs of comfort

I was unaware of the wider level of devastation to our city or the neighboring cities. Five cities had been destroyed by the high ocean water that had reclaimed the land. The great bridge to my favorite island, Sanibel, split in half and fell into the ocean. I could not wrap my mind around that.

My emotions transitioned from gratitude to grief. I was grieving for the people who were hurting, and for those who had lost everything. The ocean had opened her mouth, and swallowed everything in her path. I realized that I had survived, and again, I thought of the sense of safety the orbs had brought to me.

After eight long days, and barely any rest, the items destroyed in the garage were put out on the sidewalk. The garage had to be power washed to remove the muck. There were at least twenty pounds of dead fish in the street that were trapped as the water receded. The odor of the dead eels, and other fishes that came from the ocean and the preserve had turned our community into a stinking seaside. All the critters from the wetland preserve climbed to higher ground. There were snakes in the bonnet of my husband's Hummer for safety. For the first time, the snakes did not seem to have a message for me. They were in a fight for their own lives, and I felt compassion for their situation.

I eventually grew to understand the magnitude of devastation as the helicopters, with body bags hanging from their bellies, surveyed the waters, the wetland preserves, and the surrounding communities for dead bodies. The vibration of the sound of the choppers, and army helicopters shook the ground each time they flew by. It felt like a war zone.

My husband had returned to work for the City of Fort Myers, and was busy trying to resume water services to its residents. There was no way he could help at home. My daughter and her family were at their house on the more inland side of town where there was far less devastation. The city was destroyed in some areas, more than others. Most of the people I knew were all in similar situations as I was, so there was no one to call for help. I was so mentally and physically exhausted, and for the first time in my life, I chose myself.

After all that I had endured during the hurricane, I realized that I had not thought about work. I was not a doctor, I was a human; a woman who had just gone through a traumatic event, and I was trying to find some sense of normalcy. As I stood in my driveway, I thought to myself, "I choose me."

That day became the beginning of the new journey. I expressed so much masculine energy throughout my life's journey; I was a giver, a doer, and a life changer for others. But for the first time in my life, I needed physical help, and there was none. Sometimes, when the Universe needs to mold you, it isolates you first; a fact I was blind to for far too long.

Chapter 6:

WHEN ORCHIDS SPEAK

In choosing myself, I decided not to return to work until I regained some sense of control at home. Nine days after the toil of cleaning out the garage, I finally got to my back patio where I grow orchids. I love orchids. I normally do not remove the almost 70 orchids I own from the patio during a hurricane. They were always placed in a very strategic manner that allowed them to survive. But during Ian, the winds had been so violent and strong that, during the actual hurricane, I took a few of the plants and placed them on the ground.

On the back patio, the pool was now green from flood waters and algae growth. It was time to put this part of the house back together. I was speaking to the orchids like I had always done, and I told them, "I am going to have a conversation with Ian's parents," who is Mother Nature. I went on to say, "I don't know who raised him, but it is not nice what Ian has done to us."

I laughed out loud at the soliloquy. I was finding laughter in my own thoughts. In tending to the plants, I realized that the orchids had not lost a single flower. As I picked each of them up from the ground and surveyed them, I realized something profound had happened. All the flowering orchids preserved themselves. None of the flower spikes were broken, and none of the flowers fell off. In addition to that, it appeared that they were all in bloom. Every plant I checked displayed a new flower spike.

If you grow orchids, then you know they do not all flower at the same time. But something had seemingly happened to them. It was at that moment that the orchids began to speak to me, and I understood. I understood that they knew that a strong wind was coming which somehow gave them time to increase in strength. I finally understood that they felt the intense barometric pressure that sat over our area for eight hours during a hurricane, and it had caused them to be confused.

I paused to look at the orchids again, this time with greater depth. Who said plants do not feel? Who said that plants are not sentient? This was the beginning of my separation from intellect to a slow questioning of reality. Science has not yet proven that plants do communicate. Yet, intuitively, I knew that what I was seeing and telepathically receiving was real.

These beautifully delicate plants proved that they were in fact resilient. Despite the thunderous winds, they never broke a spike or stem. These same plants were like beautiful women who said, "look at me, but do not touch this beauty." Under normal circumstances, just handling them could cause numerous accidental damages to their leaves and flower buds. But not today. Today, they were in pain and confusion. But instead of self pity, they brought forth the best part of themselves, their flowers. And, they were doing this in silence.

They were teaching me to be strong and resilient, telling me to find the beauty in the chaos, and to dig deep into my Soul to bring out the best part of myself. I heard it loud and clear in my mind in a telepathic way. It was the same feeling as with the "knowing," but this time, it came with understanding. I turned around, marched upstairs, put on my Van Cleef pearls and my Louis Vuitton water boots, and strutted outside. I looked up at my plants and I firmly uttered, "As of today, I am going to be an orchid."

That day, I had learned a crucial lesson: never again entertain self-pity. I had partaken in conversations with these plants for years, but this time, it was on a different level of communication. The orchids were speaking back. In a moment of silence, I seamlessly entered the spiritual dimension of plants, and was not even fully aware I had transcended such a feat.

In the post-hurricane transition, my literal work as a medical doctor became more and more difficult. I was barely able to emotionally fend for myself, but so many people who had experienced trauma from the hurricane were also hurting, I had to pull myself together to be of service.

In my course of duty, I became the dumping ground for the emotions of my patients and friends. During those days, the orchids became my therapist. I told them my stories. I shared my fears, my anxieties, and my frustrations. I told them the joys of designing a new space, and the struggles with my home insurance company. The conversations about the good and the bad, about my plans, and my dreams; they heard it all.

They were the best, cheapest, and most precious therapy sessions I could have hoped for. There was no judgment; they allowed me to speak.

And yes, they always spoke back to me telepathically. I began talking, feeling, and understanding their language. One day, I was so cognizant of this knowledge, and of the ways it intensified, that I stopped to ask myself, "Can it be that these plants can communicate?"

I found myself researching communication with plants, and it led me to Hermes Trismegistus' book, *The Emerald Tablet of Thoth*. This book was how I began to understand that I was not losing my mind. I realized someone greater than I had already walked this path, and had left a trail of breadcrumbs for me to follow. The text confirmed that plants really do communicate, not only to themselves, but to us, humans. I later discovered other research in the 1973 book by Cleve Backster, *The Secret Life of Plants*. Though it is not yet accepted by the greater scientific community, it, too, confirms the telepathy of plants.

Per Hermes, there is a plane of minerals, a plane of vegetables, a plane of plants, and a plane of animals and humans. I had just consciously entered the plane of plants. This was my undeniable point of entering into the metaphysical world, and I was never turning back. I became a voracious reader of all things metaphysical. Though there was nothing specific I was looking for, I kept reading.

The months following the flood were filled with challenges for my city, my community, my patients, and family, and most of all, for me. But I became aware that I could no longer deliver or give more of myself to anyone, because I had nothing else in me to give emotionally or physically. My masculine energy was now rebalancing the feminine side of my Soul.

All my life, I had given to others, but I did not know how to receive or how to ask for help. I was always the one spontaneously helping somebody else. I was tired and in need, but, believe it or not, very few people even asked me how I was doing. The world can be so blind sometimes. There are people for whom I gave all of myself in charity that even on my worst days were still asking of me. What did I have left to give of myself? I was done, empty, and emotionally dry. But then there were friends like Laura, Lisa, and Margie who sent me strength. These women brought me healing love and support. They filled me up, and allowed me to be ready to go back to work.

My first day back to work after hurricane Ian was surreal. But as the weeks passed, my Soul was fully operating again, as it carried me and guided me, even if I never noticed.

I was increasing in strength, and I was back to having more to share. In the course of my day, I was able to better effectively take on the stress of each patient. Some people lost their whole lives; their entire home was now forever in the ocean, never to be seen again. So many people lost more than the small damages I suffered. There were endless tears and sorrow. Some people had no place to live, and relocated out of state to stay with family. As I was becoming energized to serve, I was also slowly growing spiritually. I took the opportunity to lose myself in my creativity, and began creating a new home. I could hear the "knowing," that guiding energy that sits to my left, say, "create, create, create," and I complied. I threw all my energy into the renovations of my house.

A few months before Hurricane Ian, I heard a sound, and sensed a light vibration, as if it was coming from the north side of my house. Shortly after the disaster, I became more aware that this sound had intensified, and this time it was coming from everywhere. At first, I thought that maybe it was the sounds from the generator or air conditioner, so, as the weeks went by, I gave it very little thought. But now at 3 a.m., in the stillness of the night, it was evident that the sound, a muted hum, was present and growing louder.

Early one morning, I decided to investigate the source of the sound. I listened to the walls of the house, but that was not the source. I listened to the floor, but it was not there. I used my stethoscope to listen to my heart, and I was not the source of the sound, either.

It sounded like it was everywhere, as it made an incessant *om* sound. The sound, however, was more prominent when the Universe was quiet. Somewhere between 3 and 5 a.m., when things were at its calmest, it came alive. Despite how clearly I could hear it, again, I dismissed it as sounds from nearby renovations. I imagined that the construction crew was working at night so as to not interfere with general traffic. That explanation did not make sense either because it was not exactly consistent with a mechanical sound. What I was hearing sounded like a vibration.

I remember asking my husband if he heard the sound as well, but he did not. The *om* was becoming louder and more rhythmic, and in the quiet of the nights, it synchronized with my heart beat. Instead of trying to ignore it, at 4 a.m. when I was awake, I dissolved into it. I became one with the sound. I was still deeply ignorant of the fact that the Earth was speaking to me. Mother Earth had opened her arms, and was comforting me, but I was still spiritually asleep.

The sound continued to intensify in both vibration and volume, but now I was not only hearing it at night, I was hearing it whenever the Universe went quiet. As the weeks went by, the *om* sound got even louder. It was now coming through me, causing me to hold my breath to see where the indistinguishable sound was coming from.

I am an open book, and I tend to overshare with my patients. They always leave me more enlightened from sharing my stories. Ever so often, they give me leads and insight, and I recognized that sometimes the Universe was literally speaking to me through them. That was how I found out that the vibrational sound I was hearing was called Schumann's resonance, also known as the sound of the Earth.

It is a phenomenon that can only be heard by six percent of the population. I was hearing the rhythmic vibration and heartbeat of the Earth, and it was magical. I was later informed that in some cultures the *om* is known as the sound of creation. The truth is, I was hearing with intuitive hearing.

In the months following the hurricane, the skies remained cloudless and clear, and I resumed my passion for the skies. I suddenly began to lose myself in astronomy. I upgraded my telescope and gears, and immersed myself into deep space. I was mesmerized by the beauty of the dark skies, and the speed by which the planets move when observed closely. I realized that, for many years, I had not looked up. As aware as I was that there was a sky, I stopped looking for it.

A better quality telescope also allowed me to capture better quality pictures. From the permanent station I set up from my bedroom window, I started taking pictures of Jupiter and her moons, as well as Saturn and her rings. I examined the moon, Orion, and her seven sisters. Fully engrossed, I enjoyed long nights watching the stars from my bedroom window.

Some nights, I would even climb out onto the roof and take pictures of deep space. I took pictures of Sirius, I watched the rotation of the stars, and I basked in the beauty of the Milky Way. I was also amazed by how busy the sky was, with lots of things drifting by, and darting around. It was like a busy highway coming alive in the nighttime. I thought about the same occurring during the daytime and thanked God for gravity because, for all the things flying around, I was surprised nothing fell on our heads here on Earth. But this inspired me to start researching science and physics again.

When the war between Israel and Palestine broke out on October 7, 2023, I was triggered. I experienced pain in my heart at the thought of another war. Was the world coming to an end? Just the thought of it left me so hurt. Russia was already in throws with Ukraine in what felt like humanity being caught in a never-ending destructive cycle. It all made me think of the recent memories of army helicopters searching for dead bodies in my backyard right after the hurricane.

The noises, combined with my recent flooding, allowed me to feel the pain of the people in the countries at war. I could not bear to think of how they must feel in such dreaded conditions. I was feeling the suffering of all of mankind. The empath in me had taken on more than I could bear. Thank goodness my own home was already fully repaired, and most people in the city had moved on from the trauma.

It seems as if something shifted in me, and I could not take one more catastrophe. Somehow this war forced me to examine my own existence and return to curiosity of my telepathy. Not only was I asking myself, "Who am I? Where is God in all this turmoil?" I knew deep inside that there must be more to life than this fighting, hate, pain, and suffering. It just seemed to not make any sense. The world was unraveling. I decided to seek comfort in the Bible, and that was when the rug was pulled out from under me. I felt that the foundation upon which I had built my life up to this point was shaking, shifting, and about to collapse.

I remember sitting at my kitchen table reading the Bible, and my understanding of it at that moment was nothing like I had ever seen before. The words that jumped off the pages did not make sense to me at all. When I was growing up, I read the Bible cover to cover at least four times. But when I walked away from organized Christian religion, I walked away from the Bible too. This was not with malice, but rather because I was searching for God in other places; in search of structure, if you will. My revisiting of the Bible in adulthood was supposed to be like coming home, but it was not. It was as if I had never seen what I was reading. How could I have missed all of this?

The God in Genesis appeared bitter and angry, jealous, and punitive. For the first time, I could not understand how God was so wicked, and why He would be so vengeful. It just did not make sense at all. I took a break from reading to digest this new understanding, and walked to the patio to get some fresh air.

I looked up at the night sky, and it was beautiful. The stars were out and shone brightly. To the open sky I spoke aloud,

"God where the fuck are you?

What did we ever do to you?

What did humanity do to you for you to have abandoned us in times of war?

Why would you leave us?"

I am reading a Bible full of stories about how You walk with mankind on this Earth, the same one I stand on today. You were here doing all these wonderful things, why did You stop?

61

What did we do?

Where are You?"

I was absolutely frustrated; humanity was falling apart and there seemed to be no justice.

It was now about three and a half years since the COVID-19 pandemic, and I stopped watching television; I did not even miss it. When the war became the focus for others, I retreated to astronomy. This was how I ended up engulfed in watching documentaries on historical events on YouTube. I fell in love with stories of ancient sites, and it was then when I discovered the stories of Cathars and the Zoars.

I had never heard of these things before, and I was fully fascinated. It was so refreshing to hear information that did not pertain to medicine. I was back to learning new quantum physics and celebrating the discovery of new particles I had never heard of. It felt good. It must have been so obvious to my husband that my new interests had nothing to do with my profession because he became concerned that I had lost my interest in my practice altogether. I had not. I was simply discovering the world for the first time after being a doctor for twenty-five years.

I realized that chemistry and physics had drastically changed since I was last in a classroom, and I was fascinated by the advancements. It was as if every simple thing in life amazed me. I was so wrapped in my own self discovery that I was unaware of the world around me.

It was during one of these deep dives into quantum physics that I became immersed in the life of the scientist Nikola Tesla. I was deep into the stories of his challenges, as well as his goals to provide universal energy. After watching a documentary on his obsession with numerology, I said aloud, "I wonder why Nikola Tesla was in love with the number

369?" I experienced an immediate sense of rising intuition when the "knowing" said to me, "Here, I will tell you. Write this down."

I instantly got my pen and paper, and I wrote down what I felt. I did not know what I was writing, and a week after I was done, I was still trying to figure out what the numbers, and pattern in the numbers meant. One day, I was sharing this with a patient who said to me, "it sounds as if you self-hypnotized and had a session of automatic writing."

"Automatic writing?" I asked her. "What is that?"

I had my doubts, and questioned how I could experience a trance without knowing it. I was very skewed because my impression of a trance was a person in an altered state. I researched automatic writing and had another bread crumb moment. For sure, I had experienced a spontaneous altered state, and had gone into a trance and written out the numbers which created a pattern or code. All nine numbers formed a repetitive series of numbers: 369, 258, 147. Then 111, 222, 333.

I was ignorant of numerology, and quite frankly, I never heard of it. But the patient was right, I experienced a trance.

o o o

3 6 9

o o o

| | |
3-2 6-5 9-8

2 5 8

| | | |
3-1 5-4 8-7

1 4 7

3-1 6-4 9-7
$\frac{||}{2}$ $\frac{=}{2}$ $=2$

							2	2	2

3 6 9   2 5 8.   1 4 7

| x1=3 | 3x2 | 3x3 | | 3x4 | x5 | x6 | | x7 | 18 | x |
| 3 | 6 | 9 | | ≥1 | ₱5 | 18 | | 21 | 24 | 27 |

O
10

3×0
30

| 3×₱ | 12 | 13 | | 14 | 15 | 16 | | 17 | 18 | 19 |
| 38 | 36 | 39 | | 42 | 45 | 48. | | 51 | 54 | 57. |

20
60

| 21 | 22 | 23 | | 24 | 25 | 26 | | 27 | 28 | 29 |
| 63. | 66 | 69 | | 7.2 | 75 | 78 | | 81 | 84. | 87 |

30
90

| 31 | 32 | 33 | | 34 | 35 | 36 | | 37 | 38 | 39 |
| 93 | 96 | 99 | 102 | 105 | 108 | 111 | 114 | 117 |

40
1200

| 41 | 42 | 43 | | 44 | 45 | 46 | | 47 | 48 | 49 |
| 123 | 126 | 129 | 132 | 135 | 138 | 141 | 144. | 147 |

50
150

| 51 | 52 | 53 | | 54 | 55 | 56 | | 57 | 58 | 59 |
| 153 | 156 | 159 | 162 | 165 | 168 | 171 | 174 | 177 |
*

(159)

50th block   To divide
3 block cont L → L inward is 3rd seg
= 53

The Universe speaks in math, geometry, numbers, and codes. The Divine also speaks in codes. Language can cause confusions, but geometry and codes offer no such error. Everyone knew this except me. Again, it was my patients who told me that these were called angel numbers. I went looking, and was, again, thoroughly educated. I was now trying to understand numerology.

Deep down inside, I felt like the series of numbers meant more. Within them contained a deeper purpose and a meaning. I pondered on it in every waking moment. Finally, I decided to reach out to my friend, Paul, who lived in London, and was a former college math professor. I shared the codes and design with him, and he told me how wonderful this was. He encouraged me to write a paper about it, but I told him I could not because I did not yet know what the numbers meant. He asked me how I got it, and I told him the Universe gave them to me. In response, he promptly asked me if I was okay, and if my husband was home. I knew right then that he was of no help. I was back to square one.

I was working on this puzzle for months. I gave it to friends and patients, and would ask them to see if they saw anything else. All this time, I did not know the Universe was speaking directly to me. I started searching the web, and with each search, I ordered more and more books. I worked during the day and frantically read at night; I felt like I was given a code for humanity, and I needed to discover and decipher it.

All this time, it was my personal hello from the Universe, but I did not understand that. The sound, *om*, spoke clearly to me and I missed it. Even when the Universe spoke in numbers, I missed that, too. They must have been thinking, "What is it going to take to have this girl wake up from her slumber?"

One day, it suddenly occurred to me that I might be able to find the answers in meditation. When I was disfellowshipped from organized religion at nineteen, I turned to Buddhism in search of myself. It was during those early years that I learned how to meditate. After hitting a brick wall with cracking the code, I decided I was going to return to meditation to hopefully get some insight and clarification.

In the same way I had abandoned church and the Bible, I had also abandoned meditation. In all fairness, my profession at the time left little room for personal self-development. I had not meditated in many years, and was not even sure how it would go. I had no expectations, but my mind needed silence, and I was determined to resort to any means to uncover the meaning of these numbers. I laid down on my bed, on my back with face and palms up, in the pose most comforting to me. As I settled into meditation, I remembered the challenges of keeping my mind quiet.

As the weeks progressed, I regained mind control, and each meditation session was more beautiful than the one before. I forgot how peaceful and insightful this practice could be. I began to incorporate meditations in my daily routine. I meditated twice a day. First thing in the morning, between 3 a.m. and 4 a.m., and then again later in the evening, sometimes just before bed. I rediscovered the fun in the challenge of mind control, and how much I loved it. The ease of which I fell into rhythm was like I was remembering an experience, if not a past life. I was now fully engaged.

The *om* sound was still present, now, well over three years. Although I did not hear it all the time, it never left. The intensity and volume changed, but it was ever present. At 3 a.m., I began to incorporate the vibration from the sound into my meditation process. I focused on my breath, and before I knew it, I was deep into silence and peace. I immediately began having various experiences that I would describe as pleasant. In my mind's eye, I could see swirls of colors that captivated me. I realized that I was experiencing deeper levels of concentration than I had ever in my youth.

During one memorable noon time meditation session, I was engulfed in an intense white light. It was this same white light that had consumed me when I was playing in the garden when I was nine years old. Once again, it resonated with a familiar loving presence. I did not open my eyes during the meditation to see the light this time as it felt as though I was seeing them through my eyelids. Still, I was unaware of the true nature of this light. Its presence did not bring fear, but a sense of peace.

Daytime meditation sessions are priceless. There is something about them that seems to capture energy from the Sun, and my visions are usually very clear. One afternoon during meditation, I noticed that something inside my abdomen felt like it was moving. I rested my right hand on my lower abdomen, and could actually feel the energy in motion. I was not afraid, just curious. It was not painful, but I needed to distinguish it from my natural intestinal motion. It was not gas, it was me, and the perceived motion was strong.

I was very curious about the motion in my abdomen, but I continued my daily meditation sessions. A few days later, during another meditation session, I began feeling a slight pulsation in the base of my spine. I was aware that my left foot was tingling, and there was a small rhythmic pulsation in my sacrum. With each meditation session, the energy became stronger, and more active.

It was out of curiosity that I typed into my browser why I felt like something was moving inside my abdomen during meditation. That was when I discovered Kundalini. The sleeping snake, or cobra energy of light in the base of my spine was awake and ascending. I was not prepared to discover this, and just like my thirteen-year-old self who had experienced a period for the first time, I thought that I was dying. For a moment, I wondered if somehow another person was living inside me. Although long past the age of such possibility, I wondered if I was pregnant. I visited Dr. Murray, my gynecologist, and confirmed I was not, in fact, pregnant.

Early one morning, during meditation, I felt the energy moving and pushing up against my diaphragm, near my rib cage, and in a very rhythmic beat. Armed with the knowledge that this was a Divine energy, I trusted my instincts and allowed it to find its way. The energy was intense. In its movement, it generated heat that sometimes left me in a puddle of sweat. As the weeks passed, the energy amplified, and was now behaving intelligently.

Within a few days, the energy was now at the level of my chest. It slowly migrated to just below my diaphragm, as if someone with two small hands was pushing on each side of it. I was focused on the action of this energy. It was as if a person was going through my body; moving, pushing, and tugging on my insides, fixing and stretching on my organs. I allowed it to engage out of sheer curiosity. The movements eventually made it past my diaphragm, and landed in the middle of my chest, creating a sensation of pressure. I opened my eyes and I thought, "How odd."

This snake-like energy had taken on a whole new life. In Eastern philosophy, Kundalini is a primordial energy in the base of the spine. It is believed to be the same energy that descends from the stars as a piece of the Divine light. It ignites a match of the egg and sperm, and as the fetus begins to grow, it retreats to the base of the spinal cord until it wakes up. Now, it was my time, and I was not prepared. I discovered that after the awakening of Kundalini, it transforms and unleashes the Prana life force. Per Eastern philosophy, Prana is that which gives life, and exists in the ether. Despite educating myself through reading, I still had no deep understanding of the powerful reactions taking place within me.

I guess I missed the voice of Mother Earth as she hummed to me. I missed the screams of the Universe in the numbers, and so it took the primordial energy of creation to wake me up. It engulfed me and sat on my chest. Other times, it held me down and stared in my eyes. It shook me awake and screamed, "Girl, wake up!" Something had finally grasped my attention.

Kundalini continued to migrate upwards during meditation, and during my non-meditative states, I was well aware of it. When it got to the level of my neck, it got stuck. It was, at that time, I witnessed its power. It very lovingly and gently stretched my shoulders from side to side. I swear to you, a massage therapist could not have done a better job. The energy continued to attempt to ascend despite being stuck. This was when it began to vibrate through every muscle in my neck. My neck began a slow rhythmic pulsation, and slowly progressed to a gentle shaking.

I remembered the day it finally got past my neck, and slowly creeped into my head. I could feel the pressure. Calmly, I allowed the energy to do its work. The pressure grew, and grew, and grew. I felt like my eyeballs were going to pop out of my head and fly forward. The energy filled my entire body, from my head to the skin on my face, and became a mask of electrical energy. Honestly, it felt more like a tickle than something that was moving all over.

After the Kundalini energy ascended, I was not sure what to expect. I noticed that when I was in meditations, the energy in my spine would awake and begin its ascent. During one of many such sessions, the energy engulfed my entire being with emotions of pure unconditional love. My body would tingle with love and ecstasy. The energy in this state was persistent and present 24/7. My heart was aroused, full, and bursting with unconditional love.

For weeks, my skin felt like a warm fuzzy sensation was around me. I loved everything and everyone. I was overrun with compassion for humanity. My head was in the clouds, caught up in the light from intense meditations, and my heart was overcome with love. I felt as if I was living each day in abundant joy and bliss. Quite frankly, I am surprised that I did not lift off the ground and float away.

I observed that when I went outside into the Sun at noontime, these overwhelming feelings were more intensified. It appeared as if the sunlight amplified this feeling of love, as if the Sun was hugging me in some electromagnetic way. I was aware of the physical pressure of love in my heart. As a doctor, the only way I can describe this is if something activated my vagus nerve, and its effect was manipulating my inner being, instilling a calming effect of control throughout my body. Something was changing. I had acquired a steady state of peace and love, and I was now permanently high on it. I was fully conscious and aware.

Kundalini energy was actively changing me, physically, and emotionally. I was not myself. I was well aware that although I was conscious, happy, and normal, something was changing. Like an onion, my skin was peeling off, and as I was left bare for everyone to see me. I was slowly changing, and like those snakes in my dreams, I was shedding my old skin. My patients saw the change in me and commented on my new level of apparent contentment, patience, and clarity. Still, unaware of the impending transformation, whatever was happening outside was a reflection of my inside.

For my own sanity, and just to be sure, I went to get my annual physical exam. The results showed that I was completely normal.

For those who seek to experience the same, proceed with caution. Kundalini energy is also a very sexually intense conscious energy. The cobra energy knew without question that it knew my body. Without being rude or lewd, I have never made love to a human who found all my erotic zones, but Kundalini did. Even in solitude, I was embarrassed by the experience. It was as if the energy owned this body, had come home from a long trip, and was turning on all the light switches. Slowly, all my nerve endings became alive with sensitivity in a way I had never experienced. My vagina, unprovoked, contracted with rhythmic beats.

Sometimes, during the meditation, my entire pelvis would move all on its own. I felt as if my entire body was experiencing a full body orgasm, except this was no regular orgasm. Take the best of your orgasmic experience, and multiply it by one thousand times, and then move that sensation across your entire being, from the hair on the top of your head to the tip of your toes. The sensations would not let me go. I was left with no other choice but to lay there and submit.

I also experienced Kriyas, known as spontaneous body movements. It was as if the living energy inside me wanted to do yoga and would start posing. It would stretch and move me in a rhythmic fashion, as if it knew where the tension spots in my body were, and was working to release it. This beautiful process lasted for months, and I submitted to it every time.

There was nothing frightening or painful about the entire experience. I have to say that it takes a person of strength to walk this road. It was through these personal experiences and reading that I understood the importance of sexual abstinence during this process, and how to utilize the energy for pineal activation. I was also fascinated by its actions, and over a few weeks, I noticed that with its intelligence, it seemed to find areas in my body that needed fixing, and automatically fixed it.

After the energy was fully ascended, it was very difficult to keep grounded. By grounded, I mean electrically grounded. During this time, I lost quite a number of electrical appliances in my home by just touching them. I truly was naive to all the Eastern philosophies, and the rate at which I read up on them was not in pace with the intensity and magnificence of this energy that was unfolding. As a result, it was teaching me, and my research served as confirmation of its power.

I was also speechless by everything that was taking place. How was it that, as humans, we did not speak more about this. I comprehend the spiritual concept of these experiences, but it felt more scientific. In a nutshell, a living conscious energetic electromagnetic part of my being was somehow activated by the Sun, and woke up what was literally living within me. I am convinced that the home of this energy within the psionic triangle resides in my heart, and is associated with my vagus nerve.

Chapter 7:

WISDOM AND UNDERSTANDING

I rarely consume alcohol because my gastrointestinal system just cannot tolerate it. I am not a habitual drug user, either. I tried marijuana two times in my life. The first time was when I was about 50 years old and my daughter talked me into eating a piece of marijuana cookie, and the second time was when I was on vacation in Jamaica with a friend. The first time was an awful experience, while the second time caused me to sleep all day. But each time, I felt the total loss of control over my being, so I never revisited marijuana again. It is important that I say this because what I am about to share with you is the next level.

I was still going through the Kundalini energy activation, and the experience continued to be beautiful and perfect. My heart was so full of love that I went and asked my husband to hold me. As he held me, I told him that I had no idea what was going on, but my whole body was suddenly filled with love. He said, "that must be nice." I existed in this state of being whether I was awake or sleeping. It was blissful.

I soon learned that these beautiful states were called "sidis." At this point, I was addicted to meditations. No longer able to ground myself, my head was constantly afloat, as I was deeply aware that something was changing; I was changing. I realized that this process was nothing that I was familiar with, and in my cultural experience, it was nothing I had ever heard of. I needed guidance, but I did not know where to go. Every time I thought of where I should go next, the "knowing," the ever-present energy on my left, told me that what I was searching for was inside of me. It told me that it would teach me all I needed to know.

Although I was engulfed with Kundalini energy, I never lost sight of the real reason that I was meditating: I was searching for the answers for a series of codes and numerical sequences I uncovered from Nikola Tesla. I resorted to various kinds of esoteric practices in an attempt for a solution. One time, when I was deep in self-reflection, I remembered that Jacob from the Bible slept on a stone, and was able to see a ladder to heaven. This gave me the idea to sleep on my crystal pink quartz as a pillow. Maybe, just maybe, it would somehow affect my electromagnetic energies and I, too, could put in a call to heaven. I did this for two weeks, but got no results.

One evening, it occurred to me that to get the answers I needed, I could simply ask the Universe out loud. It is almost childish saying this out loud, but, in that moment, it was like an immediate remembering of an ability I once knew. I decided I was going to meditate with the intention to involve the skies, and I was going to ask Jupiter to tell me what these numbers meant. That night, as I got into bed, I became extremely relaxed for my meditation session. Once I fell asleep that night, I did not get any of the answers. There was also nothing that was revealed to me, consciously or subconsciously, the next day. I was disappointed that Jupiter, the planet that I love, did not reveal any insights. Or so I thought.

I was not going to let that stop me. I needed answers, and as my persistence increased, I decided I was going to Sirius for the answers. Sirius is a very bright star in the night sky, and one of the closest stars to Earth. I often take pictures of her with my telescope in the early evening sky. I needed clarity and understanding on the numbers, and I felt so sure that if these numbers had a key for humanity, I needed to know. Again, I fell into a deep meditation, but this time, I was determined to not fall asleep. What felt like a brain wave shift led to a familiar jerk in my body, as I said to myself, "Don't fall asleep Marlene, do not fall asleep." As I repeated these words to myself, moments later, my life changed forever. Please understand that the journey that I am about to take you through, although I am relating this frame by frame, it all seemed to happen all at once.

I always kept my eyes closed when I meditated. This time, with my eyes closed, a brief instantaneous *whoosh* sound emanated from my forehead. The sound reminded me of pulling Velcro apart. I was not alarmed at all because I often heard sounds during my meditation sessions, similar to clicks and other snapping sounds. While I did not know what was happening, I was never afraid.

The next thing I knew, I could suddenly see the sky. The ceiling of my bedroom disappeared, and I was looking into the night, dark dawn skies, appropriate for 4 a.m. My immediate thought was that I could see through my eyelids. I told myself this because sometimes, when I closed my eyes, I could still retain the last image in my mind for a long time. But that was not the case. This experience was too new to my consciousness, and I was trying to grasp it.

What began as the dawn sky was rapidly changing into early morning. I was aware of a vibrational sound, as it reminded me of plucking a guitar string, and the reverberation it left in the air for a few seconds. I was still aware that I was in the prone position with my face up and my arms outstretched, as I floated through the skies, among the stars.

I have to admit that there was a strange sense of familiarity within this state, and it caused me to ask myself, "Where am I?" I was seemingly unalarmed that I was suddenly outside. I heard yet another electromagnetic sound, and with that, I knew I was now beyond Earth's atmosphere. The skies seemed to rapidly lighten up, and in that split second, it was now morning time.

I realized that I was not just outside of my perceived house, but outside of my human body. Floating on my back, I was still face up looking up at the sky while I drifted through the sky. The scene quickly cleared up from dawn to an early morning sky. It occurred so quickly while I was still grappling with convincing myself that I was seeing all this. I was aware that, less than a second ago, I was inside in my bedroom, laying beside my husband.

"How did I get outside?" I asked myself. As I acknowledged that I was not in fact looking through my eyelids, I could see that the trees were blowing from a gentle wind, yet I could not feel the wind on my body. I was about 100 feet from the tree but could clearly see it in its entirety, as it appeared more lemon-green in color. Despite the distance, I was able to look closely at the leaves and see the detailed internal veining structure of the leaves. It was at this moment I was fully convinced that I was in a new dimension, especially as my real human eyes had poor distant vision.

I thought, for sure, I must be dead, and became annoyed at the idea that I had somehow died. How could a healthy person die? I was not sick. I was healthy, and was just in bed. I did not feel a heart attack or a stroke or any sort of trauma? Why did I die? What was happening? I felt light, conscious of my zero-gravity state as I continued to float in the sky. It occurred to me that if I did die, I would no longer have a physical body. I decided to see if I could see my hand. I put my hand up in front of my face, and I had a hand I could see. I used my right hand to touch my left hand, and I was solidly myself. "I am alive!" But I also noticed that a small scar on my left hand between my second and third digits was not present. I knew then that the body that I was in was not my body. This body was the most perfect version of myself in both structure and senses.

I sleep naked at nights, but when I looked at my hands, I realized I was wearing a white dress with long sleeves that ended in small ruffles around my small wrist. The light fabric gently caressed my beautiful dark skin. The appearance of my hands and the style of the dress reminded me of a much younger version of myself, and for an instant, I wondered if I was immersed in a virtual game. The white dress was weightless, but flowed under me in the wind. Knowing that I was not dead, I put my hands below me feeling for the bed, but there was no bed supporting my body. This was not a dream. Not for one second did it occur to me to check my face or feel for my feet, I was floating with zero gravity, and it was exhilarating.

My location, orientation, and point of view changed in a flash. I was seeing vegetation and water below me. When I realized I was above the trees, the odd thought of not wanting to fall and injure myself crossed my mind. I realized I needed to get down on the ground of the beautiful land I was seeing below me. As soon as I thought that, I began to descend. It was magical. I instantly remembered my intention was to travel to the star, Sirius, to gather information about the series of numbers I had discovered. I had started the slow descent into the star of Sirius.

I knew without question I was in Sirius, I knew it. It would be one thing to be outside my body and my house, but to be in Sirius. How? It was light years away, and the change that had taken place had happened in a second or less. I also questioned why it looked like Earth—green, and lush with water and a captivating sky. And as I write this book, I can honestly tell you I do not recall the act of breathing in that atmosphere.

During my descent, I experienced a very familiar feeling near my left shoulder area. It was positioned a little behind me, but as it was apparent that someone or something was with me. It felt like an energy of some sort. It was "the knowing;" that energy that had been with me all of my life.

As I approached the ground, I could see the top of large trees with massive leaves. I was intrigued. I now saw the beings as they encircled and approached where I was hovering above the clearing to land. I heard them bustling against the shrub, making a sound just below me over to my right. I could not make out any clear, intelligible languages.

As I started my descent into an open area of a land space, I sensed the energy to my left floating downward with me. No language was spoken. The communication was telepathic and I was aware that the beings were beckoning me to come down. They were numerous, and drew closer towards me as I lowered myself toward the ground. It was as if they knew that I was arriving, and my presence was anticipated.

I remained conscious and self aware throughout the entire experience. At some point in my interaction with them, I was offered to stay, and I knew what that meant: I would never travel back to Earth as myself again. I thought about my husband whom I left sleeping, and I made the choice to return to Earth. Scared, I responded, "I want to go back."

The energy on my left side was still present; the one that had sat on my left shoulder with me all my life. It was an undeniable being, and in that moment, I understood that I was never alone. Up to this point, I had never physically witnessed this energy, face to face; I never turned to see what it was or looked like. I did not think I could even if I wanted to.

Then, via telepathic communication, this energy on my left side said to me in the most loving soft voice,

"Do not be afraid. Close your eyes."

After the first command, my eyes were still open because I was so mesmerized by my new environment, and was trying to take it all in.

The gentle voice commanded for the second time, "Close your eyes."

I closed my eyes. Instantaneously, I could feel myself traveling. I was moving so fast that I felt myself traveling head first back into the atmosphere of the Earth. I heard that familiar electromagnetic vibrational sound of the reverberating string. Then, aware that I was traveling through the wall of my house, I perceived the sensation of the wall on my body. I hovered over my body laying on the bed like a spaceship trying to land on a target. I lowered without any effort back into my body, and it rendered a sensation to my being similar pushing my hand into soft butter. I entered my body and felt my shoulder snap into place; first the left, then the right. *Snap. Snap.* Like a magnet, I was tucked back in place. All this happened within seconds.

I immediately opened my eyes to see that I was back in my room, in bed, and beside my husband. I touched his body with my right hand, just to make sure I was really at home. I laid there on my back in disbelief. I stared at the ceiling for the rest of the early morning trying to understand what had just happened to me. When I left Sirius, it was as night turned into day, and when I returned to Earth it was early morning. My consciousness had traversed the limitations of time and space.

To be honest, up to that point, I had no words for what just occurred. It was only after weeks of research that I discovered the correct term for what had taken place: an out of body experience or OBE for short.

I was mesmerized. I had an eye in the middle of my forehead—my own legend of the third eye. The veil of ISIS was lifted, and I was permitted to see the beyond. It was weeks before I could bring myself to tell my husband, let alone anyone else.

I cannot describe with any effective emotion the knowing that I was in possession of a virtual eye, let alone coming to the understanding that the body I had left behind on my bed was only a vehicle for my Soul. The thing that looked through my third eye was the driver of said vehicle. Spiritually, my Soul revealed itself to me. Scientifically, there are at least two versions of myself. A solid energy version composed of matter, and a second version that is also solid and made of substance that is more sophisticated, and is able to traverse matter. Both were held together by electromagnetism. As I move forward in this story, whenever I use the word 'Soul,' I will be referring to the second version of myself.

I was well aware that I was no one special, but something truly special had happened for me. I came face to face with a part of me I never knew existed. I now know that the "knowing" was my Soul guide, or a greater version of myself. In spirituality, it is referred to as the higher self. My Soul finally reminded the avatar body that it was the driver. It was difficult to prioritize what was more magical, visiting Sirius or discovering my Soul and the higher version of myself

Like the two versions of me, I realized there are two worlds separated by some type of electromagnetic layer. In my deep dive, I discovered that the second world in spirituality is referred to as the astral world. I was now a part of two worlds—half on Earth and half in the astral world. Interestingly, I felt like the Earth I came back to was the underworld, lacking in color and vitality compared to the astral world. I was back in the restrictions of my avatar body, but now seeing the world in a new way. I had re-entered the game of life from a new vantage point. I was not yet aware that this was my official initiation into a higher level of my metaphysical high strangeness.

My hunger for more metaphysical knowledge was now wide open and insatiable. I researched the third eye, and it led me down a rabbit hole about chakras. It helped me understand more about the Kundalini energy, and how it ascended up my spine, activated my pineal gland, and activated the upper chakras, through channels of energy culminating in the activation of what was my third eye. I devoted hours and hours to learning through books and podcasts. I was no longer sleeping more than four hours per day.

I worked as a doctor by day, and was a Soul detective by night. I had just come face to face with a part of me that I had no idea existed, but had been with me all my life. I now know that the energy on my left that I had sensed all my life was in fact an intelligent entity all on its own. The question, "Who am I?" changed to "What am I?"

As I settled into the understanding that I have a Soul, at first, like all humans, whatever our brains could not understand, we comfortably relegated to God. At first, I did also. But, at the time, I was grappling with my own beliefs that the God of the Bible could not be real and be so wicked, so I knew that it could not be God. I settled on spirituality with the understanding that there was some great magical thing happening that I did not understand. I began integrating the experience as fact into my life.

I began to question reality. I was not paranoid, but curiosity had my full attention. It had to be science. The out of body experience was so exhilarating that I was not hesitant in diving right back into meditations to uncover how I could have triggered the process. When it became repeatable for me that it had to be science, I now had to uncover how.

After months of research that I deemed sufficient to satisfy my brain's understanding, I bravely spoke to my husband about the experience. When I did, he said nothing more than, "uh uh." His responses always fell flat. I knew that he knew I was a little strange, but nothing like this had ever happened before. He took it just like all my other experiences—with patience and grace.

Sharing the experience with a few close friends was a little more of a challenge. Each listened in their own way, and some shared their own personal paranormal experiences with me. It was then that I began to realize that I was not alone on this journey. I grew curious as to why more people did not openly or readily share these experiences. For those of an older age group, I could see why, as the political climate of organized religion or government entities, at that time, would not tolerate it.

The beings of Sirius appeared half human in the upper part, and seemed to have four-foot-long tails ending in fish or snake tails. They were different and beautiful. When I returned, I investigated my findings. The closest thing I found was the nagas of Africa and India.

Truthfully, during my initial encounter with the inter-dimensional beings on Sirius, I was not aware of their immense technological prowess. The difficulties of inter-dimensional information transfer are not something easily explained, but are akin to taking the most recent computer information and trying to read it on a 2001 computer. It may not unbox it at all, and if it does, it could take a while, days, weeks, or even years. On my first trip, I returned with a wealth of information. Most of which changed my personal life forever, and others that left me with questions that, to this day, I cannot answer.

In one unravelled memory, I recalled a small gathering of beings who were very elegantly and beautifully dressed. I held a wine glass in my left hand, and was deep in conversation with three other beings. The room was dark, appropriately lit for a cocktail party, except it was inside a large windowless room, with rough walls that looked like uncut granite. We were being served by a person, a young lady who tripped when her shoes got caught in my long blue dress. I attempted to break her fall, but as her feet hit mine, I looked down at my own feet only to realize they were not feet at all. I had a long tail like that of a snake or mermaid. I was dismayed, and frankly, I was so shocked, too. I looked like the other beings of Sirius; half human, half reptile. I reassured myself that this was only a resurfacing memory, and was nothing more than a dream.

I returned to the initial quest; understanding the meaning of the numbers inspired by Tesla. My better understanding of Kundalini energy, along with encountering my Soul, had created more questions, and a sense of urgency to uncover the meaning of the sequence of numbers: 369, 258, 147.

For the first time since my father's death, he was heavy on my mind. I missed him so much because he, like me, was into spirituality. Just before he died, we talked about intuition, and he told me that I had been granted a gift. Shortly before his passing, we were having a conversation about something when he suddenly reminded me,

"You have the third eye, Mar."

He went on to tell me that this was why he named me St. Joan. I had never engaged in this kind of conversation with him before that day. I had always thought he was full of shit, and said whatever he thought someone wanted to hear. I realized I should have listened, but instead, I reminded him of what happened to the last St. Joan on Earth—Joan of Arc.

I was still engaging in twice daily meditation sessions, at noon, and in the evening. The more I meditated, the easier it was to fall into a deeper altered state of consciousness. I was deep in meditation one afternoon when the strangest thing happened. I was trying to see if I could make the place as dark as night, so I decided to put on an eye mask cover. I remember so distinctly going into bed to meditate with the mask over my eyes. As I went deeper and deeper into an altered state, I could feel the mask slowly coming off my face. Later that afternoon, I went so deep into meditation that I lost my awareness. When I came out of the meditation,

I was still in the bed lying on my back, face up, but no mask. The mask was neatly folded on my side table. It was one of the first times I asked questions.

"Who did that?"

"Could I have done that?"

But I had no answer. Was it my consciousness, or my awareness? Was it my Soul? Could my Soul move things? Could my consciousness really move things without me being aware? Was it the inter-dimensional beings affecting my existence? I still have no answers to this day. In many ways, the experience haunted me. It was one thing to be consciously aware of my actions in an out of body experience (OBE) in another dimension, but it was a whole other understanding to participate in an action in this dimension in which I had no awareness at the time.

If I did not do it, then who? That was the real question. In much the same way that I was able to move in another dimension to effect change, I had to question how, not only was it tangible and real in that dimension, but did this mean any entity had the ability to move into this dimension and effect change? I have no clear answers, but I am aware that something happened that day.

Later that day, when I entered my evening meditation session, I went in with an intention to ask questions specifically about the relocation of the eye mask. As I settled into meditation, I focused on my breath, and watched my thoughts. With full understanding that someone was communicating with me, I heard the melody to a song pop into my mind. It was "The Search Is Over" by Survivor.

As the song played on a loop in my mind, I was drawn to the lyrics, *How can I convince you*

What you see is real?
Who am I to blame you
For doubting what you feel?
I was always reachin'
You were just a girl I knew.
I took for granted the friend I had in you.

I was living for a dream,
Loving for a moment
Taking on the world
That was just my style
Now I look into your eyes
I can see forever.
The search is over
You were with me all the while.

I was consumed by overwhelming love, and it brought tears to my eyes. I began to sing the song out loud as long warm streaks of tears flowed from the corner of my eyes and into my ears. I had fallen in love with what I had spent my whole life looking for. I fell in love with my Soul and the higher version of myself. I now realized that this is what I was longing for when I was a child. It was as if a piece of me had clicked into place and made me whole. But the whole experience was wrapped in love. I had fallen in love with myself and I wondered if I deserved this?

My Soul was telling me that my experiences were in fact real. It confirmed to me that the "knowing," my true Soul guide, had been with me all my life. I was now fully engaged with a force and an energy in a world that was invisible to me. I was aware of its presence because of the sensation of energy around me. Unlike the orchids, this level of interaction was tangible. The Universe is alive.

When I came out of my evening meditation, I purchased the song and added it to my playlist on iTunes. I listened to it over and over and over, as I cried and cried and cried.

I started to dance with myself in the living room, freely flinging my arms around, and turning in circles with such freedom, peace, and confidence. Knowing I had a Soul that was with me, one that was living and loving and manifesting, made me feel something new. I realized that the part of me I was missing all my life was this, and now, I was complete.

I later discovered that I had experienced a mandala dance with my Soul. After my first out of body experience as an adult, I felt like an alien. The sense of not belonging was different from the feeling I had as a child. I was able to fly, time travel through the galaxies, read people's minds, discover my third eye, and I was living with conscious energy inside of me as I shape shifted and bent time.

"Who am I?" No, actually, "What am I?"

I am not a doctor, that is my profession. I am not a woman, that is my gender. I am not a wife, that is a chosen role. I am not Black, that is an assigned box, I am not African, that is my assigned race. Stripped clean of all my labels, who am I? I was finally in a beautiful existential discovery that led to my next move.

Weeks passed, and I was still in disbelief and awe about meeting my Soul, uncovering the energy of my Soul guide, and traveling to Sirius. I was so energized by this that I was constantly asking people if they knew they had a Soul. Everyone responded in the affirmative, and I was surprised by their responses. I felt as if everyone knew but me. It literally felt like I was the last person to the party. With time, I realized most people were regurgitating their beliefs, and not speaking from experience.

I was humbled by the experiences. I continued to read as much as I could, and became more informed about the OBE processes. I read Robert Monroe's research papers involving the CIA project from 1986, and discovered that the clicks I often heard during meditation were when I was in different dimensions.

I was learning to trust my inner eye, and was using it to see everything more clearly. I was able to ascend into an energy form to see the magnetic strip rolling in the cloud with images from which I received telepathic communication. With research, it had a name, and I discovered remote viewing. I read more information about the process, and discovered more about Joseph McMoneagle, the ex-CIA agent, and his remote viewing skills. The more I read, the more a whole new world opened up to me. Looking back, this was how I saw the pending flood and hurricane Helene in a vision.

It was as if, during transcendental meditation, I had floated up through the skies to get to another level. Once I did, it appeared almost like a curtain opening up, and strips of an old movie film started to play before my eyes.

I saw a hurricane that involved severe flooding. The ocean was coming onto land as the waters flowed, fierce winds howled, I saw massive mudslides, and intense destruction. I later understood this place to be the Carolinas. Having gone through something similar when I lived through hurricane Ian, I saw that the devastation was much greater than what I experienced, and tears came to my eyes. I cried, and I cried, during the meditation, and asked why I was being shown this. What was I to do with knowing so much pain was on the way?

I have come to realize that the visions that I see of the future, close or far, are not things that I can change; it is my consciousness traversing time. I now understand that these imagines all happened at once. So, there was no way to control what visions appeared or how many at a time. A few days later, after I had seen the vision, I called my friends who I knew lived in the Carolinas and I warned them of what was coming. As a matter of fact, one of my best girlfriends, Cheryl, advised me that I should come stay with her because she was more worried about Florida. I then reached out to another friend, Dr. Graham, and I told her the same thing, but I do not think I was taken seriously.

Five months later, in September, 2024, hurricane Helene landed in the Carolinas. When I saw the images of the post-hurricane destruction, it triggered my memory. I remembered the vision I had months prior. This was it. I had seen all of this before—the flooding, even the muddy waters rolling down the hillside. I recalled the roaring ocean crashing up against the land, and the heavy large raindrops that were unceasing. I circled back with my friend Cheryl whom I texted on April 15th to warn her, I reached out to my friend, Nancy, and she, too, was deep in recovery.

I reached out to many friends to provide as much comfort as I could. They admitted that they should have been a little bit more cautious. But it had caught us all by surprise. It is hard to explain a vision to most people if they themselves have never experienced one. It is even more challenging to deliver a message from a Soul not in this dimension. More so, it can be just as confusing to relay a message to a person about your awareness of a personal action or thought. Taking something from the invisible and relating it to a person that is not even aware that they have invisible parts will never resonate until that avatar becomes awake.

To this day, I continue to research metaphysical and spirituality. I was speaking to a patient who is a pastor and shared with her some of my experiences. That is when she said, "this sounds like Kabbalah." Immediately, I thought of the right friend to contact. If anyone would know more about Kabbalah, it was Brad.

When Brad and I spoke, he took the time to clarify, guide, and explain Kabbalah to me. I fell to the floor crying because for the first time, someone understood my language. When I sought deeper understanding, I ended up spending so many years going through this alone. I did not personally know anyone who cared or even understood the metaphysical. Most people often looked at me as if I needed psychological help. But the more Brad spoke, the more I cried. I lost my breath in gratitude for his explanations and his compassion.

I eventually followed the new path he had put forth before me. I was put in touch with a few groups, and started with my mystical schooling. There, I received guidance on learning about unseen and invisible forces. But these paled in comparison to what the beings had taught me directly. I discovered structured learning institutions, such as the Monroe Institute in Virginia, where one was able to learn how to initiate their own out of body experience.

When I gained deeper clarity, and read Hermes Trismegistus' *Emerald Tablets* for the second time, I felt like it was speaking directly to me because I had now lived the experience.

I was journaling heavily, and doing so sometimes multiple times per day. There were so many magical experiences to capture, and not enough time in between to properly assimilate the information. I recognized that I was giving so much time to metaphysical research that my duty to my patients could possibly begin lagging.

I was engulfed in books, with a never-ending search for knowledge. This also left little time for friends and family. Family time was a priority, and I moved into that space. But upholding shallow friendships was a challenge. My entire circle of friends had contracted over the last four years to a circle of an entrusted few. It was this small circle that grounded me in this journey. My husband was well aware of my abilities, and was giving me room in this new phase, while still being supportive. My friends, Margie and Laura listened, asked supportive questions, and learned right along with me.

Looking back, I can appreciate the way the Universe removed the energies I did not need from my life. I am eternally grateful that the Universe knew me best because I could not have grown if some people were still in my life as friends. The first contraction started with COVID, then the remainder fully contracted within two years after hurricane Ian. I spent a lot of time alone, but I was not lonely. Living in two dimensions left no time for such emotions and loneliness. This was when the orbs in my Earth dimensional life were now larger, more active, and engaging.

In hindsight, I understood that the journey to self was a lonely road. I was walking it while having so much fun, and enjoying my experiences that I never even realized I was on the road to self.

It was in that solitude when I revisited my conversations with the Universe, not only to ask, "Who am I?" but to know, "What am I?" I was having doubts about being human. I was a well-trained physician at some of the best institutions in the world, but I was never taught about any of the experiences I had. Why not? It was around this time when the concept of authoring a book crossed my mind. I figured, no other human should walk this road ignorant and unprepared as I was on this journey.

Chapter 8:

DEATH AND REBIRTH - OUROBOROS

Deconstructing the illusion of reality was not easy. It was slow and systematic. In the process, I remained in solitude, throwing myself into meditation, except for work and to spend time in my orchid garden. I was back at my orchid temple bearing my Soul. It was almost two years since Hurricane Ian, and that was the last time that I re-potted my orchids.

The orchids must have known what I was going through because they finally communicated to me that they wanted to be more like they were found in nature. So, I decided to remove them from their pots and mount them onto driftwood. At the beginning of this process, I owned about 300 orchids. By the end, I owned close to 900. Through the interaction with the orchids, I practiced being present, and living more in the moment. After a lengthy nine-month process, I converted a corner of my patio to a greenhouse. My experience with orchids blossomed, and their gratitude was demonstrated in their blooms.

One day, during the repotting process, I encountered a snake and was startled. It was wrapped around the bottom of the large driftwood that I was creating. At first, I thought it was an orchid root. But because of its location, I was able to confirm it was a snake. I used a stick to shush it, but it did not move. I was adamant, and my second beckon hit him on the edge of his tail. The tail broke off, and the snake scurried away. Just as it got under a large flower pot, it squeaked.

I was startled by the sound because I had never heard a snake make a sound before. I had no intention of hurting the snake as it was a small baby garden snake, and even felt terribly awful about causing it to lose its tail. Even as time passed, I could not get that high pitched squeal sound from the snake out of my head. I left the dismembered tail in sight as I worked around it to tend to my orchids here and there. At some point, I ran out of orchid supplies and went to the orchid nursery to grab some more.

When I left, the tail was inside the pool cage and in plain sight. But when I got back about an hour and a half later, the snake tail was gone. I was very alarmed. I thought maybe something else had eaten the snake tail, or maybe I did not leave it there at all, but I was absolutely certain that I had left this snake tail in visible sight.

I asked Richard to help me to search for the snake and its tail. We moved the flower pots and other items, but we could not find the snake or the snake tail. It bothered me because I knew I had left the snake tail inside on the patio.

I have an outdoor shower with a drain and as I turned on the water to water one of my orchids, the snake I had encountered earlier crawled up and out of the drain. As it turned to face me, it appeared wounded, almost begging for its life. Its lower half appeared to be swollen, but its center seemed swollen, too. This led me to realize the snake had eaten its own tail. I was mortified. I called Richard for assistance to move the snake to the wetlands preserve. He was equally as surprised as we both stared at the snake on the floor in front of us.

I had never heard of a snake eating its own tail, but because of the series of events that were happening for me, I had a suspicion that it was a message, or, at the very least, a sign. Based on my previous experiences with snakes, I was very confident this was a message, and its energy ignited something inside of me.

Through my research, I was able to discover that the act of a snake eating its own tail was a myth. It was not something that happened often, but should be viewed as a sign of birth and regeneration. I was still mortified by its happening because, why was I meant to live all the myths that this world could possibly offer? I felt like I was caught between two worlds, two dimensions. The only difference was that both were now my reality. In time, I began to struggle to maintain clear separations between dimensions, as I sought to hold on to my sanity.

I discovered that the mythical sign that occurred when, on a loop, a snake placed its own tail in its mouth to form the number eight was called "ouroboros." Apparently, it represented death, regeneration, and spiritual rebirth. My immediate thought was "Who is dying?", "Who is going through rebirth?" I needed to find out what it meant for me. Two years prior was the first time the orchids spoke to me, and it was also when I discovered that the Universe was interactive. Its sleeping contents laid around like spies, conscious yet silent. Now, I was confident the snake had a message for me, but I had no idea what was about to unfold.

I needed answers to all the questions leading to my existential discovery. The Universe was literally speaking to me, but my ignorance was more than I could bear. I just did not have a strong reference point to immediately navigate and interpret all that the living fabric of the Universe was throwing at me. I was blind man walking. It seemed as though as soon as I solved one puzzle, another one appeared. Like a game of tennis, I was trying to hit the ball back, but I was playing against an invisible player who was persistent.

It is funny how the feeble human brain is always in a hurry, while the Soul waits. I needed answers to all the questions, and I needed them now. My urgency was to satisfy my brain that I saw losing its grip over its reality, but my Soul was moving into position, taking authority over it, and exercising the miracles of its strength.

I was no longer the sleeping seeker. Somehow, my new position was unfamiliar to my human brain which was struggling to rationalize with experiences it had no frame of reference for in the conscious mind. I was no longer blindly following the world of illusionary constructs.

I recognized that it was nearly impossible to unsee what you know. I was no longer a programmed human, walking by faith. Now, I was an experiencer of this conscious interactive Universe. I questioned everything around me, every action, every decision, and realized how automatic some of my own actions were. While we may refer to them as "instincts," it was, in actuality, a brain-somatic reflex. As I operated from a new place within my Soul, slowing down to question what was new and unfamiliar took some adjustments. But I was on a journey that was endlessly intense, and I realized, finally, that I had no other person I knew personally to learn from or ask questions. I was going to have to submit to my Soul, and keep looking within.

For all the magic my spirit had endured over a lifetime, most people experienced only a fraction. If I were to tell anyone these recent occurrences, they would think I had gone mad. But I remained unafraid, curious, and strong. I needed help, but it was not emotional or psychiatric. What I required was help interpreting the language of the Universe. I was noticing a pattern of communication; first the numbers, then geometry, vibrations, and sounds. I chose to delve into my research and was pleased to find a wealth of information. I was confident that once I understood what was taking place, I could finally employ this knowledge, and this quest would be much smoother. But, like learning all other languages, it took time.

I innocently started this journey through curiosity. Eventually, I began chasing answers, psionics, and telepathy that led to a series of perceived codes. Though, I still had no answer for the numbers. So far, I discovered that the flesh I called a body was, in fact, an avatar. If I had just discovered my beautiful gentle Soul, what else was I missing? I was beginning to resort to accepting that I was somehow not from this Earth, that maybe I was an alien. But I also needed to know where God was.

When I began to practice meditations, the doors of communications opened up, and burst wide open, as though it was sitting there waiting for me to walk across the threshold. Taking careful instructions from the books I read, I learned about transcendental meditation.

There is a style of transcendental meditation called Jhana that became front and center of my awareness. I spent a few weeks creating and meditating on my own blue Jhana disc. I decided that I was going to go into a Jhana meditation for a deeper experience. I mastered the out of body state, but felt that there must be more. Over the last few months, I read enough books, and listened to enough YouTube videos in search of help. I was going to God in transcendental meditation, and I was not going to get out of the meditation until God told me who I am.

By this time, I had come to accept that I was something special, but could not shake the sense that I was an alien, a hybrid inter-dimensional being, if you will. I personally accepted the fact that, if I was an alien, I was okay with it. I just needed confirmation.

I have no experience with deep Jhana meditation. When I discovered meditation at nineteen, I learned that it was not the timing or how long you stayed in a meditative state that constituted its efficacy, but the intention and focus that came as a result of the meditation. There are numerous types of meditations, namely Yoga Nidra, Hatha yoga, and transcendental meditation; the ones I was most familiar with. Even within transcendental meditations, there are different levels, all attainable by the ability to focus. I instinctively knew this was what I needed to do, although I had no idea what to expect.

I spent a few weeks with my blue disc. It was advised to use my own hand to create and mold it. As preparation for my deep meditative state, I created and meditated on my own Jhana disc to help train my mind to focus. I meditated on it, and studied it for its essence. I spent hours staring at that disc. Over a few weeks, I meditated with focus on an image, and in the process, I used my mind to enlarge, shrink, magnify, and release it. I practiced how to transfer it from my mind to my inner eye. And as time passed, and with even more practice, I was able to transcend the very essence of the color blue. I could spontaneously regenerate the image on demand; a feat that I celebrated that day as a very significant accomplishment, and one even more stupendous than I had realized.

I was as ignorant going into this, as I was living. I did not know what was going to happen in this meditation, but I did not care. I needed to know if I was an alien. That day, I was determined to know.

My Aunt Veda and Uncle Roy were visiting with me, and were in their usual place in my poolside garden. They were having one of their daily loving bantering conversations. I always admired their love and devotion to each other. I looked forward to each year when they would visit me. With them both pushing their 80s, I knew that one of these trips may be my last opportunity with them. I knew what I was about to do, and their presence in the home brought me comfort and courage.

With them outside, and the house quiet, I climbed the stairs and entered my bedroom. I knew that I needed to lay my body down on my back with my palms down as this was most comfortable for me. I laid down in my usual pose—on my back, face up, hands to my side, with my palms up. I instantly surrendered my body. I could feel myself relax, and so, I closed my eyes.

I did not know how deep I was going to go, but I was going for it. As I lay there, it took a while for the Universe to start breathing through me. I started with deep breaths before I was bombarded by thoughts. I watched them float by, understanding that they were not mine. I have no idea how some of the things that popped into my head appeared there because it was not relevant; it was just energy that flew by that I watched until it filtered and withered away.

After months of dedicated daily meditation, I became familiar with the main states my body fell into. The first was where my body fell asleep due to sensual deprivation. Along the way, I felt each sense shut off as the perceived energy in me changed form. As I progressed, I felt my entire body as it slowly fell asleep as I remained conscious. As I fell deeper into a meditative state, I lost awareness of all of my five senses. In other words, as my body lay on the bed, I was unable to feel if I had been touched. I could not hear if someone walked into the room, I could not see if I opened my eyes, and my ability to smell and taste were long gone.

I was aware that the body kept testing to see if I was asleep. It sent a sharp jab of electrical current to my toes and other body parts to see if I would move, but I did not. Immediately after this stage, the body progressed into sleep paralysis. From there, the electromagnetic Soul disengaged. But even as the body pulled my muscles together like a saran wrap and bound me, I did not move. I refused to disengage my Soul. I was in this one for the end game.

As the meditation progressed, I moved into a state where my perceived body became pure energy. I kept my eyes closed, and remained focused. I quickly moved my focus from my breathing to the blue disc in my mind's eye. Now all in my mind, I had risen up into the outer layer of my being, leaving the avatar body lying on the bed beneath me.

In my mind's eye, I conjured my blue Jhana disc, and held the focus of my inner eyes to it. Working with the disc, I pulled it in, pushed it out, I made it big and small, and focused on it, refusing to let it go.

With my consciousness now fully risen out of my human body, my energetic level became a multi-layered experience where each higher level of energy seemed more refined. At the moment, I had entered my emotional energy layer. The Prana that was activated from Kundalini was now awake and alive. While I felt it flowing around me in waves of joy and ecstasy, it was a very different feeling from the ecstasy I experienced in my avatar body. Although I was not fully experiencing this through the nerves of my somatic body, it was far more beautiful and intense.

Now aware of my energy form, I was growing bigger as if the flowing energy had occupied the entire room I was in. But I knew I was not going to focus on that. I had been here before, and because it had never delivered an illumination of who I was, I knew that I needed to keep on pushing. I was here for answers, and so, I held my focus. I felt another brain wave change as I transcended from stage to stage, falling deeper and deeper into a state of being that was now unfamiliar—a stage of absolute peace and love. Time fettered away in my serenity.

The interesting thing is, I realized that the mind continues to keep a copy of the physical body that is still filled with emotions. In my emotional body, I experienced joy and absolute bliss. I was so determined not to linger in the emotions, that I acknowledged them and quickly moved on. I needed to keep my focus on the blue disc.

It was at this point that I felt as if I was in a computer game, playing against an unseen force. For a few seconds, I thought that the bliss and joy was meant to entrap me to stay at that level. It was as if my Soul was preventing me from falling for it; as if it meant to keep me focused on the blue disc.

At some point, I tasted a substance like fresh beautiful oxygen, and knew not to fall for it, either. I even smelled an indescribably beautiful fragrance that I also knew not to fall for.

In my mind, I found that I could no longer smell or see. Suddenly, the blue Jhana disc disappeared from my vision, causing me to panic. I tried unsuccessfully to bring the disc back to my mind's eye, but I failed. I felt like a person who fell overboard a ship, falling deep into the waters below without the ability to swim. That sense of terror indicated to me that something was wrong.

My mind's eye disappeared and panic set in as I lost focus. I was suddenly drawn to a faint distant sound that I recognized; the *om* sound. First faint, then it grew louder and louder and louder, until it enveloped me. The more I focused on it, the louder it became. It was the sound of creation, the sound of Mother Earth, who was back to save me. It was the same sound that I had heard for the last fifteen months. It was as if She knew that I was in distress, and She was coming to save me. Her presence in that moment was Her way of saying to me, "I got you, my child." I let go of trying to regain the visual of my mind's eye, and, instead, focused on my melodic *om*.

At some point, a sense of peace overcame me, and I leveled into it. It was a beautiful peace, and I thought I could stay there forever. In hindsight, I never lingered on the transition from sight to sound. It was ignorance that kept me going. I was unaware that my mind, just like my human avatar body, was in the process of shutting off my senses.

I ascended out of my mind, and I was now fully engaged as a pure wave of energy, and in a more refined energy state. Time was no longer present. I felt a sense of defeat as I still had no answer for the question, "Who I am." At the time, I was not appreciating the strides I made in meditation. I was so focused on my intention of self discovery that I thought, "Oh my goodness, I've come so far just to know who I was and I still do not know the answer." Almost in that instant, my mind's ears telepathically heard a voice. It was odd because, unlike the telepathy of my Soul guide, or that of the beings on Sirius, this was loud and had a different tone.

"Marlene, Marlene. I am Helen. Are you okay?" It was the voice of a young woman with a loving melodic voice.

I thought I was finally going to find out who I am. Nodding my head in the affirmative,

"Yes, yes!" I responded. "I am okay."

The voice then responded, "Okay, here it comes!"

I was not even aware that I had not asked any questions. I just thought she was going to tell me the answer to the question I came for. Immediately, a force of energy overtook me. My mind's electrical body was overtaken by a great wave of energy. It flowed upon me like a calm silent ocean wave, making its way up to my mouth. That is when my mouth disappeared.

I was shocked. I could not believe that what I sensed to be my mouth was suddenly gone. The wave had engulfed my entire body, leaving me in complete darkness. I had no body, and had no mind. I lost my "energy" self. I was now pure awareness, consciousness if you will. I entered the void and became formless. I was now one with the Divine Source of pure awareness.

I was astonished by the sudden realization that I was "no thing," or formless, but also everything all at once. I understand you inquiring how I knew this to be a fact. Though I cannot explain, the intuitive telepathic communication, the same telepathy that guided and communicated all my other life experiences, was now magnified and active. Even as the one experiencing it, I could not wrap my comprehension around what I discovered.

I was left in the darkest space one can ever imagine. The darkness was alive, moving, and aware. It was as if I had traveled into the belly of consciousness. It was empty, but full, and was as vast as a galaxy of darkness. That was when I felt as though I was expanding to occupy the infinite space. It was also when I became acutely aware that my orientation had changed. When I lost my energy body and became part of my consciousness, my awareness was no longer oriented upwards, like I was when I was laying on my back in meditation.

I began to look out in a 360 degree of awareness. In this 360 orientation, I was aware of a tiny speck of light to my left. I acknowledged the light but chose not to move because I was feeling so loved and comforted. I wanted to enjoy my current state of peace. My senses were more magnified than anything I had ever experienced to this point. As pure consciousness, I was able to see, hear, and feel. I had my emotions, and I was in a stage of awe and wonder. I tried to comprehend the experience, my new awareness, and the understanding of what was filling me. It was through this new sense of awareness that new understanding came.

I had come all this way and finally understood that my Soul was telling me that what I was trying to find was inside of me. I was searching for myself, and what I found was that I was pure awareness; not a body, or a brain. It was at that moment that I understood that the energy that was my Soul when I descended into Sirius was a part of some larger source.

I understood that the ultimate building block of all things was awareness, which was sometimes called consciousness. I was reduced to the smallest version of myself, and it was present in everything. It was while I was in that void trying to comprehend the journey to where I was that the awareness came to me. The avatar that I was only represented a

105

little piece of the whole consciousness, and I had retracted back into myself to be whole. Here I was, sitting in the presence of what I was searching for.

The "God" I accused of abandoning us, of leaving us to war on this Earth, had never abandoned me at all. This energy of awareness was so deeply woven and intertwined within me that it was me. The amnestic part of me was now back inside the complete whole. Just like the figure eight of ouroboros, I had come full circle. This was not only my death; it was my rebirth. The entire electric intelligent consciousness enveloped the part of itself, the "me" holding it with peace, love, and understanding.

The expansive energy had no gender. It was neither male or female, nor was it old or young. It had no race, creed, nationality, or borders; it was infinite. For as long as I was in it, I also had no additional identity, except a conscious love.

In a flash like download, I understood that my consciousness was infinite and without form. This was truly who I am. I clearly understood that. I then understood that everything was alive and aware, animate and inanimate. I also understood that everything came from this energy within the void. I was in the void, a darkness that produced all light, and it was surreal.

As I leveled into space, I will never forget the sense of peace I felt there. It was a different level of peace from the other levels I had entered prior. I had no idea what was next, or if there was further to go. After thoroughly enjoying the peaceful state in what seemed like forever, I figured, since I came all this way, I was planning on moving forward. At some point, I directed my awareness to the pinpoint light. I told myself they were stars, then something unexpected happened.

The next stage of my awareness was my descent out of the void, and back into an energy state. I went from being in a state of full consciousness with no form to finding myself back in my subtle energy body. I felt every moment of coming back down from the void into the matter that was my avatar body. Each layer of descent was more restrictive, from my energy, my mind, and to my flesh. I was consciously aware of every energy layer of the subtle body. Each layer added upon itself until I could no longer move; laden in flesh and laying on my back in my bed. The free consciousness was back riveted into an avatar of flesh.

I felt like I was a projection of an imagination from the mind of the Divine. From nothing to flesh, the Divine consciousness split and projected me back to the avatar in flesh. I tried to give my body enough time to ground and center itself, to wake up, and for things to assimilate. Excited, I could not wait to get up and out of the meditative state to better appreciate my discovery. I felt fuzzy, and I could barely stand up because I was still floating and felt unbalanced.

After the entire experience, it took at least half an hour to ground myself, and I was overrun by a deep sensation of hunger. I was starving for energy, even though I had just eaten lunch half an hour before the meditation. Instead, it felt like I had not eaten anything for about a week. In the act of replenishing the energy I craved, I could not eat enough nuts, dried fruits, and water.

I checked my phone and three hours had passed. It appeared that during my meditation, I spent three hours outside my human avatar. Formlessness for three hours was the first time I attempted this and for the first time, I wondered if when I left my body, if it was able to continue breathing. I could not shake the feeling like I suffered a concussion. After

I consumed some more nuts and fruits, I slept for two days after that transcendental meditation.

When I finally woke up forty-eight hours later, I walked to the patio aware that I had made a profound discovery. In that moment, when I became a conscious self-inhabiting avatar body, I remembered how, on the other side, in the astral world, I thought or imagined it, and so it came to be. As light crystallized into form, I wondered if that was what had just happened for me. I will never forget that feeling of being projected. That feeling lingered because it was how, during my unpacking, I confirmed I was a projection of light into a game called life.

As time passed, the magnitude of what I discovered was unfolding in a way that I was happy with. But, the gravity of the meaning of the discovery was beginning to mount, and with that came a new set of challenges. I went into meditation to discover who I was, but unaware that the perceived truth and information that was in my immediate consciousness was the just tip, in comparison to what was residing in my subconscious. I still did not understand how this was going to unravel everything I knew to be true to that point, or how it related to the foundations upon which I built my human avatar. This was the beginning of my deconstruction.

I went into that meditation session wanting to know who I was, and came out discovering I was an eternal, omnipresent, omnipotent consciousness playing a game called life. I finally understood why the ouroboros snake visited me. The experience of merging with the Divine as pure consciousness was my initiation. Ouroboros, the messenger, acted as the forerunner to the truth of who I am. It was trying to tell me that, to find out who I was, I would end up dying to meet my new self; the one that was going to come out of that void.

The trusted serpent had come to warn me of my pending path of death and rebirth. The snakes had yet to fail me. They were also deeply mingled in my profession as the caduceus sign in the same manner as Kundalini energy that climbed up my chakras to ignite my Soul. I wondered if our forefathers knew this information and left me a clue. Truly, the world is interactive, and there are no coincidences.

When Mother Earth first spoke to me with Her hum of the *om*, I missed it. When the water cleansed me, I missed it. When the winds comforted me, I missed it. My Soul showed itself to me as I began to wake up, but still, I was too blind to see myself. It took the Divine yanking me right back into the void before I understood who I was—a part of the Divine. I finally got it, and my life was never the same.

My experience took months to assimilate, and the knowledge took months to integrate. I could not talk about it because I did not think anyone would believe me or even comprehend. The experience made me understand what Buddha had gone through. Siddhartha Gautama, or Buddha, had sat under the Bodhi tree in the process of meditation, and would later rise up from out of it declaring a deeper understanding now known as enlightenment. It was also similar to what Jesus, or Yeshua, had shared in His lifetime on Earth; the truth he died trying to tell us. I am no "thing." I am, rather, everything, and for the first time in my life, I realized that I was enough.

I discovered that I could exit within the constraints of the human body under two separate conditions, and in two distinct forms—formed and formless. The first was into the astral plane with a version of my subtle "energy" body, and the second was into formlessness as pure consciousness. Both experiences showed me that it was not only possible, it is repeatable. It showed me that I was able to invoke science within my process.

Maybe I had died twice, but I doubt it. Part of the process of growth was discovery. In my research, I encountered cases of near-death experiences, and although similar, these were not the same. I did not die; it appeared that I was able to move my consciousness by will. The voluntary control of consciousness became my next quest. The challenge was learning the triggers and learning control.

I was finally able to wrap my mind around my discovery of my human ability to change from and to translocate consciousness. I began to appreciate that something special had happened for me, and that this was all a gift. In these states, I have travelled formless, as pure consciousness and light. This meant that, while remaining self aware, I had no body, astral or otherwise. I also learned to exist and travel as energy. While this energy could be converted into form, in those states, I traveled as a body, and not the one I had as an avatar, here on Earth.

In these formed states, I traversed the astral plane, which is an energetic copy of the current Universe in energy form, and it is even more multi-dimensional than Earth. Astral travel is a very ancient spiritual practice, and in using it, I have traversed time, both forward and backward. In my travels, I have met with other forms of inter-dimensional beings. These episodes are sometimes brief, and I do not always land in the same place.

It appears that this process was controlled by my individual vibration, my emotional vibration, and my intention, also known as psionic mind control. I was so fascinated by the process, and spoke in ancient languages that I clearly understood when I was there, but did not know when I was back on Earth. As I traveled back to this dimension, I would sometimes hit an energetic layer where both planes seemed to merge, allowing my avatar ears to experience the end of whatever event I was living in on the astral plane.

I have visited places in Antarctica, deep below the ice where I encountered a version of myself in an ice cocoon. The ice caves were active, and buried deep within the Earth. Heavily guarded, I stared at the thing hanging there and clearly understood it was me.

Beyond those caves, I have visited the underground through a hole found deep in a forest; in a place I shall never name. I have gone to a space under the Egyptian pyramids, and met with a council of nine men who taught me something I can never seem to remember when I get back. Based on their statues, they all seemed to be very important, and the room we met in was a guarded secret. I have also sat on a promontory over a grand ocean, and watched the Northern Lights in more vibrant and beautiful colors than the Earth has ever seen.

There is a way into the astral world that does not involve transcendental meditation. It is through sleep. As I relay this knowledge to you from my personal experience, I must emphasize, though, that this is more pronounced during periods surrounding healthy sustained meditation practice. This OBE can occur during sleep, and what some call vivid dreams, which are dreams that are so intense, they feel real. This is because they are real. It is real to your soul.

This was yet another point of my reality that was being torn down as I was made to believe that my dreams were not real to my brain or body. But despite this, I knew that it was real to the Soul. I discovered this during one of these periods where I found myself in an out-of-body state. It was almost as though it was a dream within a dream, and I got up and became conscious within the dream. This was an act that took much practice.

Sleep paralysis is another state of being that is very common for most people. During this state, I experienced an intense and almost unbearable vibration that allowed my consciousness to disengage from the avatar body. During these events, I was consciously aware of a magnetic triangular area that encompassed my neck and shoulder, and ran all the way to my heart for an electromagnetic release.

I walked out of one of those states into the astral plane, and onto a ziggurat. I was with a group of people who were all occupying the lower level of this ziggurat. We could see light in the upper level that flowed onto steps that led to the upper platform. I ascended those steps and could see a bright light coming from the skies above us, and understood that it was a being. As the bright, white conscious light approached the ziggurat, it passed by us with a force that caused some people to run. I did not move. I was, instead, filled with a sense of joy that they had come for me.

I remember telling someone who was quickly moving out of the way that they had come to get me. The object turned, and came directly towards us from the opposite direction, this time splitting itself into five bright orbs of light. The light joined us, and I was aware that these were conscious beings of light. In unison, they informed us that they were Arcturians from Alpha Centauri, and that the war on Orion was over, and that it was time for us to go home. They told us that it was time for a celebration, and that the Earth was to be rescued from its current state. I was overjoyed, and the emotions I felt were projected back to my avatar body, causing me to sit up immediately. I had no idea what that meant.

During an OBE, or out-of-body experience, wherever or whatever dimension I found myself in, the information I was exposed to made sense in that dimension. When the consciousness returned to the avatar body in this dimension, the understanding could become lost and require some time for it to resurface. This message I received got my curiosity going as I was uncertain if this was a past life or a current life experience.

I began to research Alpha Centauri, and found very little information, except that it was a star system. A few weeks later, while watching a documentary, the word "ziggurat" caused a trigger in my memory. It was then that I realized what I initially perceived to be a pyramid was in fact a ziggurat. Ziggurats are massive ancient step pyramidal structures that were used as temples. I searched for images of ziggurats as the one I experienced was of a specific shape. I knew that if I saw it again, I would remember it.

That was when I discovered the ziggurat of Ur. I knew that was it— I had been there. Once I began to research the structure, it revealed that it was built with an orientation toward Orion. I sat for a moment as I took this all in. I dared myself to say all of this out loud. But, us humans, we are not from Earth. We initially came as visitors due to the destruction of where we were originally from. For our safety, we travelled all over. Some of us even taught and integrated into the various civilizations we encountered. The Arcturian messengers I met came through the portal that resided in Alpha Centauri to inform us on Earth that our time had come for us to return home.

I have no immediate memory of the return plan that was laid out, but I clearly remember that there is, in fact, a plan. Like everything else, it will unfold at the right time.

From my first adult conscious memory of an OBE during my travel to Sirius to the encounter with the beings on the ziggurat of Ur, my life was a living wonder. For the first time, I realized that there is a very, very, strong and large invisible force around us; a real true to life galactic force.

To this day, I still travel to other dimensions. Though, at times, I have no idea what I am doing, I remain fascinated by it all. I am curious and determined to learn, and because of this, I am aware of my Soul conscious during these out-of-body experiences. Other times I have found myself out-of-body with no recollection of initiating the process. Sometimes, I harbor suspicions that I was being abducted by the inter-dimensional beings, but that was when my own self discovery took on a whole new level in this game called life.

Chapter 9:

THE ILLUMINATION

I am forever reminded that most people physically die before they can experience what I have. I am humbled and grateful for the opportunity to experience this while I am still alive. I am even more grateful to be able to courageously walk myself into the void and experience oneness with the Divine consciousness, and to be able to do it at will. The information I learned took a while to completely unfold, and to be honest, it is always still unfolding.

After the void, I immediately began the painfully slow, long process of integration. I immediately began to assimilate and integrate the information I was given by taking the subconscious knowledge to the conscious, and matching the pieces to my daily life in a way that made sense to the current reality. As the weeks and months passed, and I apparently integrated in slow bits, I lost the sense of fear. This was followed by the loss of all emotions of hate, anger, judgement, and unquenchable desire. Well aware of what constituted these emotions, I no longer experience them. I grew to become more cognizant of positive changes occurring in the operation and function of my somatic-brain body in this dimension.

I often wondered if I died the day I entered the void, and the answer is yes. The little energy that I am was engulfed by a much bigger force. Not only was it symbolic, it was therapeutic. I was never the same human after the void. I was resurrected with a sense of wholeness. I further discovered that each time I entered the void, it was not a resurrection, but a refining. The better control I gained over my emotional being, the more strengthened my Soul became.

After months of assimilation and integration, I went through a period of anticipation. I was always asking, "What is next?" My awareness grew rapidly, and the expansion in my consciousness was vast. It took some time for me to better understand that I was not going to "escape the grid or the matrix," as some put it. All that had truly changed was my vantage point. I was now leveling back into the game, and as I did, I continued to be taught by the inter-dimensional beings of Sirius. My daily existence now took on new teaching and learning opportunities. On this path, my Soul guide never left, and was also joined by a host that constantly taught.

I was shown the truth about the infrastructures of our institutions, and the paradigm shifts that happened about three thousand years ago; events that forced humans to be blind seekers. I was shown that there were plans to end this state of being, and that the galaxy was an active dynamic breathing being that wove and intertwined with us, right here. The Divine, the Universe, and all the parts of the Divine consciousness that existed in it wanted this slavery that humanity is caught in to end.

One afternoon, I was overcome by fatigue and fell into a deep sleep. My awareness brought me into the astral plane. This time, I was well aware that I was existing within a vivid dream, and in a controlled way, I was able to step out of the dream and into the astral plane. I was on a very modern craft with a grey metal platform, and I was among many souls who were listening to a speech being delivered. I was by no means confused about anything taking place. I was aware, and fully understood the message.

Something the speaker said made me become emotionally excited, and, suddenly, I was back in my avatar body. When I awoke, I was still able to hear and speak the ancient language. I wrote out what I remembered, and have since somewhat figured out parts of the message. I did not understand the language prior, and the voice was certainly not that of any human language I had ever heard. Though I can speak the language, I am unable to spell it. But if I were to try, it is along the lines of:

"Arun Qinton Kaah."

I am not sure what it means.

I sometimes laugh at myself and wonder if my house is a portal. Then I remember that the events happen for me everywhere so, no, it was me. I am the portal. I can see how spirituality can drive someone into insanity, because when you discover your true self, you are not the same person you once were, and you can no longer see the world through the same eyes. Everything about reality, as you know it, begins to dismantle.

A few months after my encounter with the awareness in the void, I hit peak exhaustion due constant research. I found that I needed an extended period of rest. I could no longer keep up working as a full-time medical doctor by day, while performing as a full-time spiritual detective at night. There were not enough hours in a day to do both tasks. I began planning a long one-month vacation. I recognized that I needed uninterrupted rest to integrate. Integration is a slow process of accepting information received from another dimension, and consciously or unconsciously putting it into functional application into daily life and life events in this dimension.

Up to this period in time, I was integrating well, and thankfully, I was not in the mental ward. This was great progress compared to my namesake, Saint Joan of Arc, who was burned alive at the stake for examining and speaking the truth about reality in the way they experienced inter-dimensional communication at the time. By this time, I was well aware that the lessons I learned were messages and enlightenment, not just for myself, but also for others. I realized that, in order to speak more openly about my experience, it would take time. I was confident in my truth, but it also required something more tangible than a series of experiences.

I am extremely clairvoyant, clairsentient, and clairaudient. Operating in this state is so intense because I can feel the emotions of others, and hear the things they do not say. It is more amplified than being an empath. Constantly having to keep that energy in check leaves me exhausted.

I was also intrigued by the things I was discovering about the Universe and myself that I could not keep it to myself. I tried to share my experiences with family, friends, and patients, but I could feel their palpable doubt. They looked at me as though I had just absolutely lost my mind. I had gone from being a sane doctor to a seemingly insane schizophrenic woman in their eyes. I saw and felt the energy of pity from those around me.

Due to these overwhelming feelings of wanting others to understand my message and concepts, I bargained with the Divine, and that was how I was granted a single glimpse of the magic within myself. My format of education also changed, and I was given the illumination.

One evening, I told the Universe, "I need a breakthrough, or I am going to have a breakdown."

In a moment of compassion, telepathically I heard, "You are tired. Go to bed. Come back at 3:00 a.m. and I will show you something."

I said, "okay," and went to sleep.

At 3:00 a.m. the next morning, I woke up and put on my red robe before hustling down the stairs. If the Universe was going to show me something, I had better be prepared to see it. I grabbed my glasses in one hand, and my phone in the other to take pictures, and went out to the patio. I looked around and searched the skies for about five minutes, and nothing happened.

Over time, I became intensely clairsentient. I was able to feel the energies around me, but that night I felt nothing. There was no communication, no energy shift. Nothing. Needless to say, I was a little disappointed. How could I have misread those strong feelings of communication between the Universe and my Soul? Sadly, after waiting and waiting, I decided to go back inside.

As I entered the house, I received telepathic instructions to look at my security camera. I thought it was really strange because why would I do that? I got into bed and began to search the security video. I was not prepared for what I was about to see.

As I watched the footage, I saw myself looking around, waiting with my hands akimbo. I had my phone in one hand, ready to take pictures of whatever I saw.

During the wait, it appeared as if, just as I rocked my body to the left, a spark of white light appeared from my lower back. It was bright and radiating from my being. A few seconds later, there was another flash of light, then another. By now, it was a little higher than the first, as it ascended and intensified into a large white plume of light radiating from my body. The light that started in my sacrum had climbed in a zig-zag-like fashion, and was now radiating from my heart. I was turned toward the camera with my head facing the sky so I did not see any of the lights flashing with my naked eyes. I felt no heat and no motion. As it ascended and expanded in diameter, it finally stopped at the level of my heart before it disappeared.

Watching this living light engulf me left me speechless. I was trying to understand what it meant. I thought for a moment that some alien had shone a light on me from the sky. After integration comes clarity, and I understood that I was pure light. My light body had been activated, and it was as if I had been granted a glimpse of my Soul. I have the ability to transform from pre-electrical energy to pure light. My human Soul was manifesting the very essence of it being in this dimension. It demonstrated to me that us, "Huemans," are composed of energy and light. The human Soul is a conscious intelligent being, and the Soul can create wonders if we allow the brain to get out of the way.

I showed the video clip to my husband, and he said it looked like lightning had struck me. I asked him if he had ever seen lightning strike the same place five times, and he had no words. I have shown the clip to numerous people, and no one had any words. I have since called this experience "the illumination."

This illumination is what led me down another rabbit hole where I discovered the Merkabah in Kabbalah. This was a spiritual belief that the body was made of light and energy, and that humans, over time, activated this light vessel in a process of awakening. Here, the inner kundalini energy ascends through chakra and nadis, displaying small imperceivable electrical channels located within the body, and in the energy field surrounding it. The understanding offered me a sense of relief. The Universe, my guides, were right. Going out in the night to use the camera was the only way I would appreciate the electromagnetic energy my own human eyes could not see. My Soul knew that night I needed the video evidence, which I now use as a saving grace for the people who thought I had literally gone off the edge. Later, I was able to use the security camera to capture some amazing inter-dimensional beings and plasma orbs activity.

My education from the inter-dimensional beings continued, and I was shown how the orbs as plasma exist within a fabric we call spacetime, and that we refer to as air. I spent many days learning, documenting, and teaching anyone who would listen to me. One evening, one of the beings appeared as a large plasma ball. They normally move very, very quickly, so I was asked to obtain the security footage to slow down the film, and I did. Upon doing so, you could clearly see the warping of the media we call air, but to them, it was known as space time or the ether. It contained water, light, plasma, and energy. I was informed that it was this existing plan that Nikola Tesla was shown, and was about to capture; an experiment he was unable to finish.

I was shown that the formless state in which I cannot see myself was my true appearance. Intuitively, I knew that when I got my brainwave better trained, I would be able to tap into this fabric with intent, and with a more defined outcome. This is already what we do via manifestations, but I will avoid the subject of manifestation, as advised by the beings.

The physical geometric orientation of my home is that the front door is located in the west, and the back is located in the east. Therefore, it is not uncommon that my mornings are graced by the rising Sun in the east. One morning, I walked out to the patio and noticed the rising Sun, and for reasons I cannot explain, it held my attention. It was as if it knew that I was still in awe of the discovery I had made a few hours ago where I shone like a lightning bolt. I noticed that the Sun did not appear the same way to me at all. I was looking directly into it which was now a shiny silver disc, surrounded by a ring of white light. It was hurling itself through the sky, dancing and bouncing around. I was so mesmerized; I could not break my gaze.

As the Sun danced across the sky, I saw a purple haze of an energy arising from the bottom of the Sun that slowly grew to form what looked like a loose shadow of a key. It captivated me. As it rose, it got larger. It eventually sat on top of the Sun for a joy ride across the sky. I have since come to know this key as an ankh. The ankh is a part of the essence of the Sun. It is something I see all the time, and sometimes the color changes to orange or purple, but it always starts out orange. I gazed into the morning Sun for 15 minutes; it was beautiful.

It took a voice from behind me to break my gaze. It was my mother. She must have noticed my fixation on the Sun and was concerned. She walked up behind me to ask what I was doing? I told her I was just looking at the Sun. I did not elaborate because by now I had come to realize that no one else saw the things I did. We both stood there, side by side, but even in that moment, she could not see the symbol riding on top of the Sun.

I was always told never to look directly into the Sun because it would hurt my eyes. But that morning, I was able to see it clearly for the first time, and witness the beauty of its being. I felt something that day. It calmed me so deeply that I slept for six hours. I still have a beautiful dance with the Sun. It, too, was alive, conscious, and aware of my existence. I felt the love it radiated at me.

Later that week, I encountered the rising Sun, this time, with a green haze. It was a beautiful thing to behold. I now understand that there are no coincidences in life so I went digging for the meaning of a green Sun. It was then that I discovered the ankh and its relationship to the Egyptians and ancient religions. The symbol apparently represented the key of life. It was a symbol that indicated mortality and resurrection. Additional research further went on to explain that this symbol often represented the Sun's path and horizon. I am going to differ with this wisdom, as the ankh is the essence of the Sun, much in the same way my physical body has a Soul.

Ever since that day, I have developed a closer relationship with the Sun and the ankh. I still Sun gaze, as it is one of the most wonderful ways to start my day.

To be honest, as I write this book, I am equally in amazement. The process of self-discovery and the ultimate interactive nature of the Universe intrigues me. I discovered more about myself than I care to admit. During the process of integration, one of the things that happened to me was a process of remembrance, almost like moments of Déjà vu with past experiences. I realized that my experiences with these inter-dimensional beings were not new. I also became very suspicious that I had been monitored by them all my life. I thought about the day my mask was removed from my face and placed on the side table during my meditation. I thought about the many times I found myself out of body on a ship, or the one time in particular where I found myself adrift on a dark craft. During my OBE, I telepathically received the instructions,

"Close your eyes. You are going home."

Instantly, I closed my eyes because there was a sense of familiarity with the beings. I did not see them with my eyes, but I knew that they were present. I also knew the energy signature to be the ones that had visited me all my life, since childhood. I could clearly recall the time I was on a craft in a silver suit with other people listening to a speech of some sort. It felt as though I was a part of some galactic force, living two distinct lives. I realized then that I was an inter-dimensional novice.

In the most recent past, I had an out-of-body experience where I relived the descent of my Soul into this lifetime. The instructions that I was given upon my descent into my mother's womb was, "Keep fighting against the dark forces."

I heard the voice loud and clear. I waited a few weeks for enlightenment and clarity, and when it did not come, I got frustrated.

This was what led to a long conversation with the Universe and the open sky. I asked the inter-dimensional beings to show themselves. I expressed my frustrations with what appeared to be a one-sided relationship. I also asked that if I were to ever be abducted again, let it not be against my will or in a state of amnesia. I demanded clarity on my memories and the memories I apparently had erased. I asked for clearer instructions, and reminded them that my vision was poor.

I acknowledged their presence in the sky when I saw what appeared to be their craft at night, but I was not able to tell for sure. Honestly, they seemed to always be present, as they would sometimes dart in the sky, from north to south with intense speed, then stop and wink at me. Each time, it brought a smile to my Soul.

A week later, at approximately 9:45 p.m. on June 9, 2025, I was driving back from a restaurant. I was in my car with my daughter, Rochelle, my thirteen-year-old grandson, Landon, and my granddaughter, Serenity, who was seven. I was a mile away from my home, heading south on Winkler Road when a slight motion caught my attention from my left peripheral vision. As I turned to look at it, I recognized the jet-black triangular craft clearly visible against the full orange moon lit sky.

It was a UFO. It was surreal. I immediately alerted my grandson to look at the object. It was approximately 60 feet wide, and approximately 8 feet high. It was cruising at about 10-feet from the ground and nestled among the trees heading toward my car. It traversed the street with its lights dimmed, and appeared to swim slowly towards our car. I could clearly see that each corner of the equilateral triangular shaped object had an orange red light in the corner of each triangle. The three-dimensional sides had smaller green LED looking lights all along the sides.

The craft approached me and my initial heart's reaction was, "Oh, it's you!" I knew them. There was a sense of familiarity I could not shake. The craft approached and hovered just over my car. I stopped driving and looked up in time to see the extended spoke of the triangle hanging over the window on my side. The craft exited from hovering above my car to the right, and as I looked at it again, I noticed that it seemed alive, almost fully aware and conscious.

The craft was as matte black as the void. Despite the orange moon in the sky, it reflected no light. There was no sound emitted from the UFO, and it passed through the trees leaving them unaffected. It also passed through the electrical power lines on the street above the car and the power was unaffected.

My family was now agitated and shouting for me to drive off. I wanted to get out and take pictures, but their well-being at that moment was more important. I knew there would be more opportunities for that to come. The triangular craft slowly slid off to the right, rotated twice, and jetted away at high speed. The most interesting thing I observed was that the craft itself was alive and conscious. Its soft gliding motion reminded me of watching a large stingray maneuvering in water. I did not see any occupants inside the craft, but the sight of the craft brought back memories of the night I woke up on a craft and was told to go back to sleep because I was going home. The calm sense of familiarity I could not ignore was because it was this same craft.

My family witnessed an amazing, magnificent event up close and personal. When I watched the craft operate, it reminded me of my body passing through matter, leaving surrounding matter unaffected. I think the craft, similar to the astral body, was made up of neutrinos; a much finer substance than electrons, protons, or quarks.

My family needed to witness this with me. I think the beings needed them to understand my experiences. I also needed that visitation to finally close this message out to you.

I will tell you this again, yes, a galactic force does exist. I am humbled to be able to communicate with the beings, though I had no idea my exercise would result in this level of response. As the craft disappeared into the darkness, I knew they would be back.

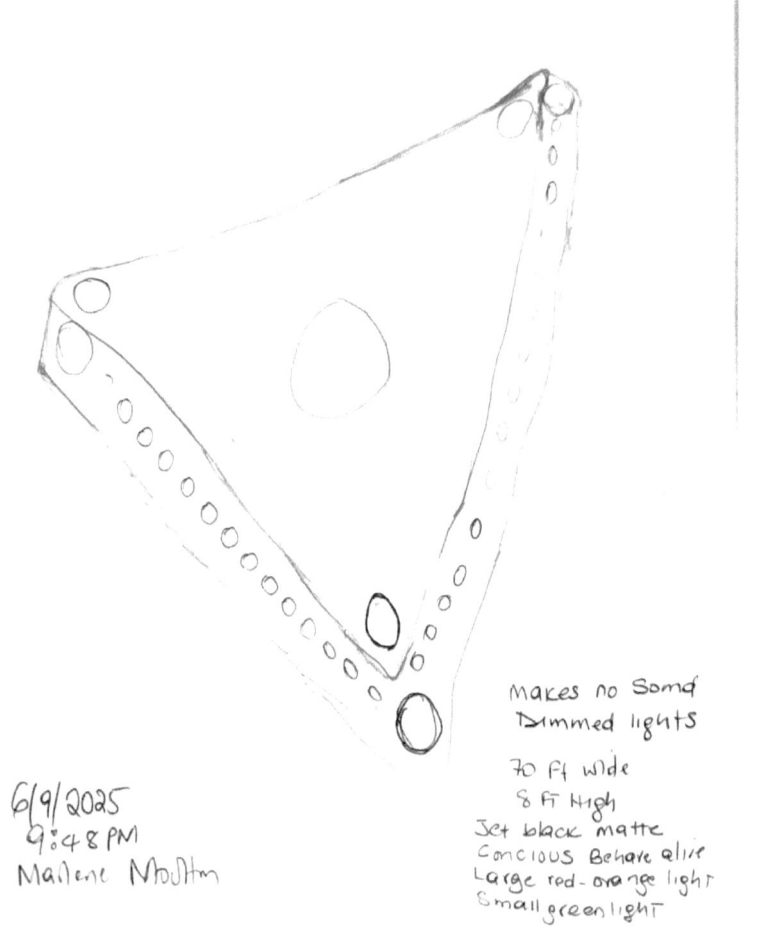

6/9/2025
9:48 PM
Mailenc Nboultm

makes no Somd
Dimmed lights
70 Ft wide
8 FT High
Jet black matte
Concious Behave alive
Large red-orange light
Small green light

Illumination is light and sight, and it would only be prudent to discuss my third eye here. If you can recall my spontaneous assumption of seeing through my eyelids during my first OBE, it was because I truly felt as though I could see through my eyelids. After seeing this black craft,

I cannot help but think about how I was able to see the craft among the trees using peripheral vision, and without the need to turn my head. But it was more than that.

Although I was not even in line with the craft, it was as if while approaching the area, I saw it before I could see it. I recall that it was as if time had slowed. I remember questioning to myself, "What is that?" while still advancing the car as I drove home. It was only when I was in line with the craft that I then turned my head to see it with my eyes. That sequence of events bothered me, and I could not stop thinking about it. I knew that I must have seen it with my Soul, but how? I went online to research it, and found a video of a little boy seeing while blind folded. I wondered if this was what had happened for me.

I first noticed this vision anomaly during meditation. I can say for sure that it was after kundalini awakening. Whenever I closed my eyes in meditation, I noticed that after a while, I would see light. This inner light was more pronounced during daytime meditation, and at night, I would see the light from the fire alarm, a small green light in the ceiling. I usually squinted my eyes tighter to close it, and noticed that it created an entire short burst of light all on its own.

One afternoon, I covered my eyes in the daytime and noticed that my peripheral vision was in fact active. I was surprised, but really not surprised. Later that night, before my meditation session, I used teraderm to seal my eyelids shut. Approximately 20 minutes later, I entered the typical relaxed brain wave alpha waves which were now accompanied by visual swirls of colors and light. This caused what looked to be an internal light.

Over time my peripheral vision became more active, and with effort and mental focus on my right eye, I was able to attain slight vision in the right upper vision field. It started as a small hole, and widened with time to allow for a clearer viewing area. The vision itself appeared at first like shadows and light, but with more training, it became a clear vision that could be used for limited reading. I have better long range vision in this mode, compared to my natural vision where I am nearsighted.

I covered both physical eyeballs, and this did not affect the third eye vision. The real vision comes from between my two eyes. I have identified a small area of skin that, if covered, renders my third eye vision void. This area is not in the forehead as depicted by spiritual diagrams. This area might be photosensitive, and therefore require more research to better clarify. After a session of viewing the world from this third eye, immediately after, I noticed that my natural vision that was nearsighted was very poor, but returned to normal within a short time. I think about how perfect my eyes were in my first OBE, to the depth where I could see the small veins in leaves of trees 100 feet away, and now I better understand the blessing of the Soul.

I wonder what we used this for as humans in the past, and, at the same time, wonder if this was some new feature for us to use in the future. It is this Soul vision that I seemed to use in remote viewing and visions because what I saw was so very clear. So, it may actually be a future psionic feature. This was quite the surprise for me, as I can now better understand how to also use this internal light.

This vestige of sight is seen in some animals, fish, and reptiles like tuataras, lizards, salamanders, octopus, and some fish. I might be overreaching here, but it made me believe the beings on Sirius had left us the original blueprint for humanity. Some of the beings I encountered were half human with reptilian lower bodies, while others had human upper bodies with bodies of a fish for their lower half.

I have always had heightened senses, and use it in my work as a doctor. Most illnesses have an odor, and it is very pronounced. Illness like sore throat, skin infections by certain bacteria, sinus infection, and even COVID has a distinct putrid odor. I am excited to add this new vision to see where it leads.

Chapter 10:

EARTH WATER WIND AND FIRE

Over time, as I share my story with others, some mention that it sounds like a DMT (N,N-Dimethyltryptamine) or ayahuasca experience. But I have no experience with these drugs. The assumption did make me wonder if I had some chemical inside of me that was creating these experiences. Out of sheer curiosity, I had a brief moment when I wanted to try ayahuasca just to compare it to my own prior experiences. Before I could complete the thought, telepathically, I was reminded by my Soul that I did not need those drugs. It reminded me that everything I had experienced was from me. It was enough.

If there was more knowledge out there, my Soul was going to teach me everything I needed to know. The knowledge I gained from books was supportive and served as another perspective, but my Soul told me that what I was searching for was inside of me. The message was loud and clear.

My long-awaited vacation to Machu Picchu in Peru that I had been planning for the last five months was drawing near. With this new information, I was excited to go, but I had a feeling that I was never going to go on that vacation. After a long period of mental integration, I knew I needed a break, so in the summer of 2024, I decided that Wednesday, July 31 would be my last day at work. I was going to be taking a month off.

I had been working since I was nineteen years old, and I truly had no idea what it meant to rest. I always said I would rest when I died. I wanted to take time away from work to continue my inward journey, without distraction. My staff suggested that I work out the remainder of the week until Friday, but something inside of me knew that Wednesday needed to be the official start of my vacation. But that's not what the Universe had in mind.

On my last day at work, I started the morning with meditation. My energy was good and positive, and it was that energy that I brought into work with me. But, as the morning progressed, I started to feel a sense of heavy, negative energy around me, and I did not know where it was coming from. It was an energy that I had never felt before. Normally, if I sensed negative energy from another human, I immediately knew the difference, even if I did not know what it was about. But this energy was not that. The only way to describe it was as a sense of dread.

For a moment, I thought maybe it was the office building, but that was not it. The negativity was so intense that I could not focus on my work. I told my assistant, Kelsey, about the feeling of intense negativity. Over time, I had been able to share my experiences, insights, intuitions, and OBE travels with her, without judgement. So when I told her what I was sensing, and that I needed her to cancel my schedule for the rest of the morning, and reschedule the afternoon to televisits, she understood, and made it happen. I did not want to abandon my patients, but I just thought if I got out of the building, the negative energy I was sensing would dissipate.

I quickly worked through my morning schedule, and as soon as I was done, I jumped into my car and bolted. By now, the energy was at an all out peak, and I needed to get away from it as fast as I could.

As I pulled my car out of the parking lot, I was about 30 feet from my office door when my phone rang; my daughter was calling. The feeling of negative energy intensified, forcing me to not want to answer the call. Overwhelmed by emotional pain, I said to myself, "I cannot take anymore of whatever was happening." After a few moments, however, I took the call. It was my daughter, after all, and I could not abandon her. The second I answered the phone, petrified, she exclaimed, "Mommy, my house is on fire!" As we spoke, her house was engulfed in flames.

Immediately after she uttered her painful words, the negative energy I had felt for the last three hours dissipated. I instantly felt my energy release, leaving me in a state of exhaustion. Before my transformation and self discovery, I would have been anxious, shocked, surprised, and wailing. But I was not. I was calm and relieved. I realized that the vacation I so carefully planned, down to this day, was not for me. It was time relegated by the Universe for me to spend with my daughter and her family.

The Universe knew I needed to be off. In an instant, my daughter, her husband, and my two grandchildren had become homeless, and the Universe knew I needed to be there for them. After the chaos settled, I remembered documenting April 15 as the day I had a dream in which I saw a house on fire. It was so lucid, it scared me. I physically went out to check the outdoor kitchen, and all the gas lines in it. It was then that I found that I had left a warming drawer on, and was able to turn it right off. But now I know that was not it. The scene of the fire at my daughter's house was what I had seen in the dream.

There is something to be said about the scientific theory of entanglement. Over the years, my own living energy had become so deeply intertwined with my daughter that I can no longer know mine from hers. For three hours that morning, I was in agony for her, not me. I felt it coming. When the negative energy was mounting in me, she was in those moments pulling her children out of the house to physical safety, all while securing her family and pets.

The emotional scars it left behind were the parts that were not foreseen, and that, for all of us, was the beginning of a new chapter; a new challenge in our lives. The dark night of my Soul was now unfolding. But, how much more could I possibly take?

After much investigation by the city fire department, we suspected that the fire had started from the battery of an electric bike she received as a gift from a company which had self-ignited in her garage.

Despite the chaos taking form around me, I tried my best to hold on to the numbers I had discovered as my chasing of these answers had been the thing that brought me into meditation in the first place. One day, after I was meditating at the poolside, I looked up at the sky and thought about those numbers. I settled into meditation, and began to visualize them, bringing them front and center in my awareness. Over time, it became easier to find clarity through the practice of meditation. I would turn my focus into a question, and allow the answer to slowly float from the unconscious to the conscious. Suddenly, it occurred to me that the numbers were a frequency in hertz. The purpose of the numbers is for DNA repair.

When that revelation hit me, I opened my eyes and saw approximately one hundred birds fly over my pool cage, moving in flow, as if dancing with the wind. It was clear that the Universe was celebrating the closing of a cycle.

The Universe was reaffirming what I had just understood, and said, "She finally got it!" It dawned on me to record it, and I was able to capture the experience on my phone; for two long minutes, they celebrated with me and it was amazing.

All discoveries happen at the right time. The numbers were important, but the purpose they served would not have made sense to me at the beginning of my journey; my mindset was not there yet. I was awakening, and the Universe knew that after awakening, the physical human body underwent a transformation; a progress that was encoded in the DNA.

Certain frequencies in sound, be it in music or in nature, facilitate this repair process. The frequency triggers the DNA to initiate the process to begin the up-code and decode, each frequency affecting a different step.

This information is not new. Sound has been used in healing for decades, to facilitate sleep, alleviate pain, and rebalance energy.

The 369 frequency is considered the God wave. Some use it as 936 to accomplish the same effect. 258 or 852 have the same healing effect on our DNA. Finally 147 or 741 was meant for peace. In the same vein, 111, 222, or 333 are used in numerology, and are considered angel numbers. However, through research, I found that different people see one or all of these numbers during a time when the Universe is communicating with them.

Finally, my major questions had been answered. I asked myself, "Who am I?" and I found myself deep inside of me. I also asked myself, "What am I?" and discovered that I am Divine awareness; part of a beautiful Divine spirit. Understanding these numbers brought me closure.

Chapter 11:

COMING FULL CIRCLE

CONCLUSION

Through the series of experiences which happened for me, I assimilated and integrated the information I learned from my own experience, along with direct guidance and experiences from inter-dimensional beings. Hence, in this chapter, I will convey my interpretation of the lessons from experiences at that time. I am aware that I am not the only person who has ever experienced expanded states of consciousness leading to enlightenment or has seen and appreciated the world for what it is: a digital hologram. But maybe, in this modern age, I am one of the few willing to document my eccentric experience and share it with you.

I am not religious, and as you can see in my delivery, I avoided fancy spiritual terminology. I only interjected some terms throughout in order for you to clearly follow my thought process and the journey. My intent was to deliver my experience exactly the way I traversed it, from the point of view of a novice.

I am not some special or perfect human; these experiences are my birthright as much as they are yours. They are experiences that you are capable of right here, right now, if you understand how to utilize your mind. Do not wait to be some religiously perfect human as, frankly, there is no such thing as perfection. But the point I am trying to make is that, if I am allowed to experience these moments, you can too. I did not spend a lifetime planning this process, I just lived in my best light, and remained true to myself serving humanity.

I feel vulnerable sharing this journey as I do not know how people will perceive me, nor I do not care. This is my truth, and I know what I went through, what I saw, and what I heard. I am hoping that my experience becomes an inspiration for others to experience the true interactive holographic world we all live in.

Looking back, I can see the inner strength it took for me to walk this road and grant myself grace. I appreciate how spirituality borders on the edge of insanity, but I survived so far to overcome fear, hate, anger, judgement, and desire. It took strong will to not fall apart as the living fabric of the Universe became alive and interactive around me. It took courage to help me understand myself when I discovered that I was a projection, and saw my body erupting in flashes of light on my security camera. With every step, I have embraced my new perspective in this game called life, and as I continue to play, it unfolds.

I share my honest experience with you and I refuse to hide behind a pseudonym to do so. I refuse to paint my experience as fiction, and, as a medical doctor, I refuse to continue to operate in ignorance or deceive others of their birthright to greatness. We are more than just a pound of brain and flesh. We are a part of Divine light; we are pure energy. What we see in the world through our eyes is pure awareness and consciousness. I believe in science, and though limited at this time, it is the only modality we have to maneuver or group knowledge through this Universe. If I were not inspired by the psionic and science, I would not be so affected to take the time to share this with you.

The term "God" is coined by man. A word used to mean something greater than ourselves. As humans, whatever we do not understand, we relegate to God. We dare any inquisitive mind to question God, and instill a sense of shame in anyone brave enough to do so. This is ignorance. They demand that we be satisfied with our ignorance by questioning if we have faith. They take it one step further and collectively categorize any experience that cannot be proven by conventional science as spirituality. But one day, science and spirituality will merge.

Based on my personal experience, what I consider to be God is a conscious energy force, and fundamental building block of all the things that reside within us; both animate and inanimate. What is considered to be a spiritual awakening, I will call a growth in awareness or consciousness. It is a change instigated by biochemical and electromagnetic processes that allows us to experience the world from a multi-dimensional perspective.

These processes are very heavily controlled by the ability to control the energy field called the mind. The abolition of fear, and the discipline and relaxation of the individual mind are vital to achieve that state, and it happens only through meditation. It is important to point out that you are capable of all of these things, and more. Do not get trapped in the brief experiences that pills and drugs offer. They are not reproducible by you, and in time, they will be used to control you, and more importantly, it will eventually cause attrition in your natural ability and intuitive instincts.

I was unprepared for the knowledge the Universe unleashed upon me. I researched what was happening for me through varying media. I searched for knowledge like the pieces of a puzzle, and each time I engaged, they brought me light. This search vivified an understanding that the truth, life, and divinity are present everywhere, and in everything, demonstrating true omnipotence and omniscience. The process of fully understanding awakening, and the expansion of consciousness, all while anticipating next steps is not easy. So, that is why I am advocating for a more structured way to teach every human this truth; in a manner that is simple, free, and not tied to religion or politics.

We have methods for increasing intelligence, measured by an intelligence quotient or IQ marker. We measure our emotional progression by EQ, or our emotional quotient. But we also need to implement processes for developing our psionic intuitiveness through a psionic quotient, or PQ. This educational structure needs to be in place before this version of our human vehicle, also known as homo sapiens, ascends. In our ignorance, we see aliens as threatening only because we lack comprehension of their technology.

It is because of this same ancestral ignorance that we have in the past referred to them as Gods. We are very capable of progression, but we are limiting ourselves by the mental bondage of the ignorance we practice in religion and education. Truly, just like the Matrix, ask yourself, "What spoon?"

As the world does not exist in a permanent, tangible form, the shortest distance between two objects is, in actuality, not a straight line.

Because of this, you must learn how to bring the object to you by bending time. Scientifically, we call this quantum jumping.

We frequently experience the holographic world, but we dismiss the experiences. This is because the brain automatically gives us a familiar frame of reference. Have you ever gone into a room to retrieve an item you securely placed there moments before, but upon entering the room the item is nowhere to be found? You then become persistent in the search for the item because you are certain it was placed on the table, for instance, just before you left the room. In that moment, you would be correct; you did place the object on the table, and when you returned it was gone.

This occurred because the digital hologram did not repopulate the item. If you were not alone in the room, you would strongly believe that someone had stolen it or relocated it. I learned from the inter-dimensional beings to repopulate in two ways: simply step out of the room and re-enter it to facilitate a more complete regeneration of the holographic matter that your brain can perceive, or simply close my eyes and look at it again. One of those two ways will always work. While we are in the process of better understanding this process, I suggest you read up on the experiment of Schrödinger's cat.

Upon traversing the metaphysical learning process, known as a spiritual awakening, and discovering reality as a holographic illusion, I went through all the stages of grief. At first, I was in a quasi-denial that quickly moved into anger. I was angry that the movies had me laughing at myself. Movies like Alice in Wonderland, and The Matrix are wonderful reflections of our multi-dimensional reality. In many ways, they very closely reflected some of my own experiences. Yet, I was angry that I was hoodwinked by an illusionary life, and the infrastructures. How could I not see it? I considered myself very intelligent, so how could I miss it?

My Soul, that little piece of the Divine, reminded me that intelligence needs to be applied for one to have wisdom. I granted myself grace, but also cried my heart out. How could I miss so many opportunities to wake up? How could I have sunk so far into this game of life that I lost myself and no longer knew who I was?

Today, I am finally in a place of acceptance. Through this acceptance, I have a better understanding of the brave writers and producers of those films, and the risks they took to deliver the message to us. They had a lot to lose if the message of reality was delivered in any other way. In the era and climate that they spoke, their credibility, profession, and reputation would all be at risk. Our government is well aware of all that I documented here, as they have conducted research centered around this in the 1950s. This research is now an open document available to us known as "Project Stargate."

Over the decades, they have continued to use psionic in ways unimaginable to us. For more information on this matter, research voice to skull, and V2K technology. Some of the very technologies sold to you are your own capabilities dumbed down. You are far more magnificent than you are even aware. The government training programs used to train a selected few to have enough information on psionics to be able to render a formal educational training program in schools for all humans.

Seeing the world through the eyes of the Soul breaks the illusion of reality, and delivers the truth with clarity. Yet, it softens the harsh blow as the foundations upon which I built my old world crumbles. My Soul conveys a compassionate delivery, allowing for grace when integrating new knowledge that leads to deeper wisdom, and allows said wisdom to lead to understanding.

Most near-death experiencers, which should really be called death experiencers, will tell you that they left their bodies before the impact of whatever caused the trauma leading to their potential death. So many people and their experiences cannot be wrong. I have never experienced a near-death, so I cannot elaborate, except to use it to substantiate my point. I will repeat there is no death.

If I may clarify here, when I say no one dies, I am merely acknowledging that death is a transition door; a symbolic point of exit from this holographic game called life. Where the energy changes form, and our loved ones are on the other side in whatever form they chose. They can be disembodied as light, exist as pure energy, or as a formed body, just not the one composed of carbon and minerals as we are here on Earth in this dimension.

I was guided by inter-dimensional beings in the delivery of this book. I may follow in the path of my namesake, St. Joan of Arc, and be burned alive at the stake for speaking this truth. I can leave my body behind at the end of the game, even surrender to so-called death, but there is no death, the same way God is not anthropomorphic, and I am "no thing."

I returned from the void with no sense of fear. I felt totally free, understanding there is no death, and for the first time in my life, I began to live when I understood that no one dies. Of all the experiences I shared with the Universe, experiencing the void had the most significant effect on me. I am a different person; becoming one with the Divine left me whole.

"I am enough," is my mantra for this phase of my life. I am so complete and content that there is nothing in the world I need. I completely lost the sense of desire for material goods because the Divine is with me all my life, and that is enough.

I am humbled and honored to be a part of something so great. I am not going to be judged by an angry God. I do not need to be a part of a special race, creed, nationality or club to belong, I was no heathen or gentile. I am powerful and eternally enough.

I am living with a new sense of freedom, as if I climbed a mountain top and staked my success flag at the peak in my old world of illusion. But now, I am on my descent of the mountain to face my new reality, and because of this, my vantage point has changed in this game. I discovered that the purpose of spiritual growth and expansion of consciousness is not to exit the illusionary matrix, but to better negotiate it once you see it for what it is: to face the world, if you will.

Waking up to an expanded consciousness is a journey, not a destination. Up to the point of transfiguration and emergence, the curiosity that drove me along the quest was beautiful. It is the aftermath that is painful. Shattering the illusion of the world is painful and powerful, yet shocking. I investigated every belief I used to make my former identity, and I pulled them apart and released them. These included my religious beliefs, my formal education, and my emotions. Tearing down and rebuilding myself was when the dark night of my Soul began.

This dark night was the beginning of reckoning life's past trauma and pain. I was breaking down old beliefs and recreating new ones to close out my old unresolved emotions. It led me to release shallow relationships, and create new ones that supported the growth of my Soul.

I saw myself from the inside out, and had to painfully accept my shortcomings in order to fix them. I saw my beliefs, my assumptions, judgements, my reflective actions without thought, and all the things that had to be removed in order to heal.

Healing is a process that has to be lived, and actions and energy that need to be extracted and purged. It is painful. I could not imagine that after all the love I experienced walking with the Divine, I was left to face such darkness. During this time, I truly felt alone. Telepathically, I was reminded by the higher version of myself and the inter-dimensional beings that I was never alone. As I rebuilt myself, I built, not just a new body, but a new identity in a new world. I am living from my Soul, upon a platform where the Divine is writing my truth, wisdom, and understanding.

This rebuilding phase is the most challenging because, sometimes I feel as if I am in the old world with old beliefs, and other times I transition back into my new consciousness. It is a constant subtle shift. I do not automatically accept input from my five senses or my emotions, but I have learned to sit back and examine every input to my senses. To do so, I found myself having automatic phrases that I had to utter, or automatic emotions that were triggered by certain words with no reason at all for the resulting emotion.

In short, I was able to see my body-brain on autopilot. It was then that I began to gain control of the body-brain complex I inhabited; the one that I believed was me all my life. Do not get me wrong, I love my body. It has served me well in this game of life. Unlike some gurus that teach you that the body is not you, I agree it is "not you," but do not hate it. Love it, integrate it, and it will love you right back, and even more when you gain control over it. After all, without it, you cannot remain in the game. The goal is integration of the Soul as the driver, and the body as a vehicle. The body is as programmable as anything else that has a hard drive. If you do not believe me, read the CIA project on MK ULTRA conducted from 1953 to 1973.

My inter-dimensional guides explained that the body is a vehicle. When we occupy our car to travel from point A to point B, we do not become the car. In the same way, you, the Soul, is the driver, the awareness energy that occupies the body. Our avatar body is only a vehicle, and therefore should not be something to cling to or personalize. But due to misinformation, us humans have misidentified the body as a person, as the "I."

The beings further explained that there is a way to decipher the body from the Soul. The five senses of the body require contact in order to be activated, and the electrical impulses gathered are interpreted by the brain. The computed information is projected to your mind as the energy layer around your body leads to an experience. The Soul has a copy of the five senses, plus the sense of intuition. These intuitive senses do not require direct contact to be activated. You know when you are operating from the Soul when interactions with your mind result in an experience where no direct contact is involved. I discovered this to be true when I was able to see my surroundings while blindfolded.

At this new level of consciousness, it is easier to see through all the smoke screens in the world; a world I thought I knew, and in which I woke up to find myself a slave. I was unknowingly a slave to materialism all because of a disease developed from a misdirected search for external energy. My forefathers freed themselves from slavery, and I lived my life

147

believing that I was free. I woke up to realize I was never free. This slavery, however, is voluntary, and therefore, I have the power to release myself by becoming a more responsible consumer of the Earth's resources.

I have embraced my experiences while peeling back the layers of my illusion and trauma. Like orchids that sometimes abandon healthy roots for a while and spring new roots in a different direction, similarly, I have moved in the opposite direction of everything I believed I knew of this world to be true or "truth." There were no "trues." Like a pendulum, or a sine wave, I am now riding the tide of the Universe, perfectly in sync. Whether giving up, giving out, or giving in to Her; I have sprung new roots.

This journey allowed me to break through my second early childhood trauma: poverty. Wisdom and understanding liberated me from that painful experience, and I was finally able to let it go. I grew to understand that I was always enough. My Soul recognized that I transcended the trauma, and advised me daily to get rid of what no longer served me. I cleaned out my closets and sold everything. I no longer needed the designer items that filled my closets; from Birkins to Chanel, Gucci to Louis Vuitton. I did not need them anymore.

It was as if these items that once represented symbols of success were secretly my personal shame. They were screaming loudly, "Look, she fell for the hoax." I owned Chanel bags in every color of the rainbow, and now they were all gone. Of all the Birkins I owned, I was down to just one. Though I have not lost my sense of style, I lost my desire to consume. Anything I did not already own, I did not need. That included the yacht, the airplane, and everything else. I recognized that I was, and have always been, truly enough.

My friend Mark, a jeweler, was confused when I showed up at his store with a large box of jewelry made of fine gold and platinum; a lifetime of precious and semi-precious stones I had collected over the years. I released them so that they could serve as something beautiful for someone else.

I realized that I am a creator, and that I was hoarding all these things because I was addicted to creating. My Soul was a never ceasing energy that in my most innate form sought to create. I was in love with the process of creating "the new." Designing "a new outfit," creating "a new space," making a beautiful table setting for dinner with friends. My Soul taught me that creation never ended, it ebbed and flowed.

The ouroboros snake taught me that the beginning was the end, and the end was the beginning. Because of this, I learned to love things without possessing them. I learned to love and leave them the way I found them because it was all me. I did not need to make them my personal baggage to prove a point. I spent more time with a better balance between creating and simply just being. Creation fed my mind, and meditation fed my Soul.

I divested old real estate properties, commercial and residential, that cluttered my life. I sold everything but the essentials of my home. Even that was too much for me in my new state of awareness. I was living in the moment, and trusting my intuition to remain in the flow of the Universe.

When I traveled to the astral plane, I took nothing with me but my crystal clear memories and emotions. So, too, is the reality that we leave this Earth with nothing but memories. Memories of love, experiences of self-love, time spent with your family, friends, all the things you loved unconditionally. I was surprised to realize that in any dimension, I was able to retain the same energy signature, regardless of appearance, and never forgot my experiences on Earth. So, moving forward I demanded that they be good ones, and positive ones wrapped up with love.

One day, the Universe was testing me through Serenity, my granddaughter. We were lying on the bed together when she asked, "Grandma, of all the things in the world that I need to learn, what is the most important?" I paused for a second, looked in her eyes, and I told her, "Love. Love everyone unconditionally, and with all your heart and Soul. Even on the days when it is hard to love them, keep loving them. That is the most important thing to learn."

When I remembered how I commanded myself to retreat from the skies in Sirius, I realized just how powerful my thoughts could be. Whatever I thought, I instantly created in that dimension, and created with my mind. This was a game changer for me when I returned to Earth. In other dimensions, creation was instant, while here on Earth, the limiting factor was time, and our entanglement with others. There was heaven, but there was also hell because we created it with our minds. Therefore, I continued to see the world as a beautiful dynamic atmosphere, one in which my interaction created my own existence, and experiences. It was this power that we used to harness tactics known as manifestations.

When I emerged from my spiritual awakening transfigured, I did not have a vestige of my old self. I was a different human being. A being that operated from the heart, and not the brain. This is something that I cannot fully explain, as it has to be experienced. My center of operation shifted, and the brain took impulses from the holographic environment I thought and knew with my heart. But then, I was reminded that the word emotion meant "energy in motion." I was committed to staying positive, and expressing gratitude while actively transmuting negative thoughts or emotions. I consciously exercised the power of the will. I learned that we could live in any emotional state we chose, but we had to learn how to move the energy from our field in a process called transmutation. This was done by a process we often call, "fake it til you make it." It involved exercising the power of the will to put in motion the emotions you wished to attract or release.

With time, I lost my ability to feel anger, judgement, and hate. I was never not pious, as I knew what constituted these emotions. I just no longer experienced them. This opened up my ability to see myself in others, and let me use the world as a mirror to my state of mind.

Through integration, the information I learned took a while to completely unfold, and, to be honest, it was always still unfolding even as I wrote this book. I am sure that if I travelled the road to consciousness under the guidance of a spiritual Guru, I would have had a better understanding of my expectations. But, instead, I was living the lessons as I went, patiently allowing my Soul to guide me. My very independent Soul wanted it this way. In hindsight, I would not have wanted it any other way. If I spent my life preparing for this discovery, I very likely would have waned in my eagerness and lost interest with time.

I understood that I was operating from a place of knowing, and not operating from a place of faith. It gave me confidence, and at the same time, humility. I learned how to balance that confidence by having compassion for people around me that were still spiritually asleep or better yet, left in a dream. They were still the Divine force enveloped within an avatar not yet awakened.

I exercised compassion when I watched these sleeping avatars wreak havoc on each other, and on this world. I held space for them because I hoped one day, they would see that what they were doing was not to one another, but directly to themselves. Truth is, one day they will see it, and the realization will leave them in an imaginary hell. We are all the same consciousness; the same that looks through the eyes of all things.

One thing I learned was to meet people where they were, and not to see them for who they could be. In the clinic I operate, I met some wonderful young people who worked for me. I now realize how much pain I must have caused them over the years. When they came in, they were so smart and full of energy. I saw them many years in the future in a profession that I thought they would excel in. I saw for them a glory they were unable to see in themselves. I pushed, and I pushed, and I pushed for them to grow and be "better" until I pushed them away from my company, and out of my life. I judged them for not being enough as they were, not recognizing that they were on their own Soul journey. I was literally pushing everyone to fit a belief system with an image of success that I was trapped in. I thank them for the role they played as a mirror to that painful defect in my own psyche. Their existence in my life taught me so much.

I have also forgiven my mother who abandoned me in childhood. As a young girl in a complex relationship, I cannot be sure what I would have done myself. For that reason, she lives with me to this day. I love her immensely, and in that love, I seek to protect her from any further abuse as she ages. Finally, I thank the student in middle school who told me I was poor. It was the turning point I needed to fuel my success. To the architects of my stable foundation, Aunt Veda and Uncle Roy, my only child, Rochelle, and to my husband, Richard, words cannot do it, simply, thank you.

I am living the meaning of the name of my practice, "The Listening Doctor." A name coined telepathically, and it was no coincidence. All the years that my intuition was involved in the telepathic process, it was my Soul listening to my patients. I now save space for patients to speak, and I listen even when I know every word they are about to say.

To everyone I have cared for in my practice, just know that you are a part of my Soul family, and have somehow agreed to be a part of my self-discovery. As I slowly harness greater intuition, and the energy that these experiences have granted me, I hope to continue to serve humanity in new ways, wherever it leads. I see myself starting fire in my hands as I learn to bring the energy of chi into this realm. I plan to use it to heal myself and others. After all, that was always the Divine plan.

Applying the truth that there is one consciousness (non-duality) took some work on my part. There is only one great mind. I am aware that the pure consciousness that I am is the same consciousness that looks through the eyes of all other humans, and all things in creation. This is the same consciousness of those who can freely move and those who cannot. All things are conscious, all things have the essence of the Divine in it. There is no us or them. I am in the birds in my backyard, the orchids in my garden, the snake I encountered, and even the cup of coffee I enjoy; I am all of it, and so is Divine awareness. We can call it God.

As I write this book, I am still interacting with the Universe, and encourage you to never miss a message in your daily interaction. I am visited by a blue jay almost every day. This bird has allowed me to come close and sing to it. I have not yet broken into the essence of the bird. A few days ago, I was in traffic and maybe the same blue jay perched on the passenger side mirror of my car as I drove in traffic. I was so blown away by the moment that I took pictures. There are those that will say this was a coincidence, but I have learned a long time ago that there are no coincidences. Instead, I looked up what its presence meant. It meant to speak your truth. I also remember how the kundalini energy was blocked at the level of my throat and worked so hard to get through.

This, I later discovered, was because I needed to speak my truth and be sincere. So, here I am in that sincerity. It took the whole universe to wake me up from an amnestic sleep, but now I have personally experienced traversing a slow dance with the force of every element of this Universe.

The journey to self is arduous and, for me, it took the primary governor, the Earth, and Her three forces or elements—water, wind, and fire—to initiate my spiritual awakening. It took the Sun, the Moon and the Stars. They all gave a part of themselves to reconstruct me, and it took them all coming together to wake me up from my spiritual slumber.

Mother Earth was the first to call me with her *om*; that beautiful sound of creation. She whispered in my ear for months, and I missed it. We all know that the presence of water is powerful and cleansing. During Hurricane Ian, the blessed water was the first of Her forces to come to me. When I opened the garage door and I saw the water, as it climbed the stairs, I fell to my knees and surrendered.

With Hurricane Ian came the Earth's second force; the wind had destroyed the house, and shook the walls around me. The power of the wind embraced me once I surrendered.

It was the grace of the Moon that, in the deep darkness of the night, used the opportunity to show me the light that I am as my Soul erupted into bursts of light. It was the Sun that danced and spoke to and through me as its energy and my energy became one.

When orchids speak, I listen. So, too, did the animal kingdom with that beautiful baby snake, ouroboros—the message bearer of my own impending death and rebirth. Yet, when they all revealed themselves, I was still too blind to see. It was the inter-dimensional beings that motivated, insisted, and guided me to clarity, and with them, the story is ongoing.

My patients, family, and friends through whose lips the Universe used to speak directly to me, rendering clues and answers; to them all, I say thank you. But, finally, it was the force of fire that sealed my Soul. The fire burned my daughter's house down, and in it, the fire symbolically cleansed and healed a force of light within me during the phase of the dark night of my Soul. When this cleansing, awakening process was done, like an unprocessed nugget of gold, I was shining. Like an oyster, I turned my painful grains of sand into tears of pearls. I am whole; one with the Divine.

Kundalini energy is still ever present, and is in a new form of flow. My entire body is electrically charged all the time, and the new intelligent conscious life force within me feels like I have inherited a new organ made of energy.

My whole body feels like living electricity is coursing through me and is always charged and actively firing. I can tell the difference between my internal electrical motion and the energy in my external fields. I feel like the life force energy crawls around and recharges each cell, and most of the time, it sits active on the top of my head, and between my eyes, at the third eye. My constantly charged body had blown more electrical equipment in my home than I care to admit. But, since then, I have learned how to ground myself daily by going to my garden temple to interact with my orchids.

As a practicing medical doctor, I was taught that the brain does not think, it computes. Though my body was shut off as I lay in bed, and apparently no longer breathing at some point, I remained conscious and able to think. By medical terms, I would need to be consciously present in the body to breathe. In other words, if my consciousness goes somewhere else outside of my avatar, and into some other dimension, does this mean I am in both places at once? Does this have anything to do with the physics concept of entanglement? I can confirm that when I am in an OBE in any dimension, I am fully aware and engaged in that dimension just as I am here on Earth in this dimension.

Although I am aware I live on earth and have a body, I do not see the avatar body-brain complex, nor do I engage with it until my consciousness returns to it. Other times, in an OBE, I am well aware that in those states, I can perceive the body lying on the bed, but again, I am consciously outside of it.

I want you to grant me grace as I try to find words to explain an experience and a reality that for me has no words in our current diction to bridge the gap. We are still in a world where "proof" or objective evidence dominates our reality, and what is not seen does not exist. This belief is a programing downfall for humanity. In science, it believes that a dark hole is a lack of energy, and a lack of light when the truth is that it is the opposite.

Science believes that if you enter a dark hole, you cannot come out, or you must exit the same way you entered. Just as science still tries to grasp the concept of quantum entanglement, it is also trying to prove God; a notion that will never happen. The Divine is no "thing" to be proven, but one to be experienced.

The vehicle called the body operates like any other software. As time passed, and my data was downloaded, slowly unzipped, and uploaded, I understood that the Universe I was living in was made of small triangular pieces constructing a spherical holographic matrix of activated light and darkness. When the activated light was crystalized, the energy formed an imprint in a fabric that some call ether, and we call matter. This fabric also exists around us, and we call it air. However, what we call air is a magical mix of water and plasma energy and consciousness.

The beings demonstrated the concept to me on my security camera, and I was able to clearly see it using my limited vision. This was the energy source that Tesla was aware of, and was trying to harness.

Today, we are advancing in a world that, one day, the volume of energy we need to support the artificial intelligence, AI, we create will collapse. If we do not understand and harness zero-point energy, our civilization, like all others, will collapse. A year ago, I told anyone who would listen that one day the United States would attack Iran. As I write this book, the story has begun. Let me share with you what the beings told me.

The United States, under the guise of war, will attack Iran and harvest their nuclear energy. That is the primary focus. The secondary intention is to destroy the tablets that our history as humanity were written on. They used this same strategy to attack Iraq, harvest nuclear energy, and destroy their historical items. They will travel the world, and instigate the same tactics with Russia, North Korea, and China. This crazed effort to harvest nuclear energy will manifest when our governments try to get us civilians to vote for the use of nuclear energy as an energy source. Despite our trepidations, and knowing the right thing, they will convince us that it is best for us. But this will not be tolerated by intelligent beings with whom we share the Earth.

The last time our civilization utilised nuclear energy, we used it to destroy ourselves and the Earth. It was the intelligent inter-dimensional beings that terraformed the Earth, making it habitable as it is today. I repeat, our future is zero-point energy, which must be free to all.

The Bible is not a history book. There are many truths in it, and some brainwashed wickedness disguised as the loving Source we call God. In Genesis, it says God created the Earth, nothing new was created, and what was present was reorganized. It says that He utilized what was already there, as the waters parted and the land resurfaced.

In today's scientific world, we have a term for that: terraform. In the same way when a rib was taken from Adam's side to create Eve, it is not magic. In today's science, it is called grating and cloning. It is our first pre-civilized documentation of cloning. Do not be shocked that we did it to Dolly, the first sheep we cloned in our lifetime. All I am getting at is that, in the dawn of our civilization, when we had no words for the magic we witnessed, or the magic that the inter-dimensional beings who made our vehicle body-brain complex were, we called them "God." But they are just like us, one consciousness, one awareness, and a part of one great energetic awareness. Notice I did not say anyone made you, you were not created. You just are. You existed before this world, and forever will exist.

The world is constructed with rules that govern the game of life. The only force unmeasured is our will, and that is the de facto force that creates all the probabilities and possibilities. I do not pretend to have answers for all my experiences; I am not here to debate or discuss everything I have seen, but rather to share with you a journey and the experiences as to how I discover that I am living in a multi-dimensional world. I have progressed to a stage where I can seamlessly traverse dual dimensions within my normal daily life affairs, and I see the way my brain is giving up its dominance I think more with my heart. My Soul never sleeps, and it never ages as it teaches me wisdom.

Who better to tell you about this crazy experience if not me? I could not have written this story myself; it took the Universe to help put the words of my experiences together. There are inter-dimensional beings living with and among us. Call them aliens if you wish, but I avoid the term as I find it to be degrading. Extraterrestrial means additional land-living beings, so please stop saying extraterrestrials while looking upwards to the sky. I have encountered them, and interacted with them. I am grateful that my daughter and grandchildren have also had the privilege to share the experience with me on my last encounter. They are varied, and I feel safe in their presence.

I realize that they are us. They are from different star systems, and so are we. The human body as previously mentioned is a vehicle, and it is what inhabits the vehicle that is our unique signature. Be cognizant when you interact with others, and ask yourself who is driving the body vehicle.

Although I have no regrets about the way I have lived my life, if I had my awakening, expansion in consciousness earlier in my life, I would play the game of life in a very different way. I would live like a monk, and spend my days with the Divine in whose presence there is eternal peace. But we all will return to that state. Instead, I accept and appreciate my role in the greater plan. I understand that every time I came close to waking up before falling back into the external search as a consumer, my need for materialism was all a part of the great work. What an orchestration. The timing had to be right, as there are things to accomplish, and inner growth and experiences shared before the initiation.

How do I prevent myself from sinking so deep into amnesia the next time around? If I ever decide to play this game again, I want to find a cave and lay on my back and meditate every day. I would turn away from work, as the years of working until I die have passed; all I want now is to be.

There is so much to experience in this world, and we cannot do it all in one lifetime. I realize I came into the game of life as an old Soul, playing in a modern era, and I am grateful for that. I look back and see the dots clearer now. We are immersed in a game called life. The beauty of the game is waking up to who we are. Earth, this planet, is a school or a place of learning, and life is a game. It is a university called "the Universe," and we are the players, blinded from a part of ourselves, or our magical soul.

The purpose of the game is for us to have experiences through a process of creation. In this process, we discover the hidden part of ourselves, our Soul. At that time, we wake up and begin to live and love.

Playing the game called life on Earth is not easy; but it is one worth playing. I am delighted that I found ways to play it to the fullest in this lifetime. I am hoping that, in the next time, I return to Earth when the "aliens", or inter-dimensional beings, would have arrived. Until then, let us continue to play, and be sure to find me in the void when you exit this game called life, and get to the other side. Playing this game seems like years during the game, but it is really only a few minutes back home in the stars.

This game of life is addictive. You will have multiple opportunities to play this game over, and over again. It is something we have come to know as re-incarnation. I can hear you now saying that you will never come back to Earth again. And you will each time we tell ourselves we can do better. When we do, we lay out better plans, and better paths to awakening. We engage with new people, and the starting point of amnesia always seems to win.

I find humor in the structure of this game called life, and how, despite all we learn the first time, each reset wipes us clean, allowing us to do the same experiences all over again; enduring outcomes that are just a hair different from the first time. Thank goodness for the brief moments of Déjà vu that remind us that we have done this before. This is why I have a message for you, so that you can better understand who you are in this lifetime.

Remember, it is a very addictive game, and like anything else, you will get better at it the next time around. Your search for knowledge has led you here, and for this, you will be rewarded with the answers you seek in a message for you, as told to me. After all, I am here to reveal the secrets needed to help you start your own journey within. So, keep going.

Chapter 12:

THE MESSAGE

I am serving as a medium for the delivery of a message from the Universe, through inter-dimensional beings. In this section, I will abstain from my personal opinions and conjecture. The primary message here is that, as humans, we need to discover who we are. We are pure awareness, and we are powerful. Our failure to understand this is keeping us in material slavery, and is resulting in destruction of the Earth and each other due to our greed.

I am not religious, and have no formal training in religion or mysticism. You may ask, then, why am I writing about a topic in which I am no expert? I did not choose the story to be told; it chose me. I am not here to challenge your science, religion, or belief. My wish is to deliver these messages in a way that leaves you informed and motivated to find your own state of unity. My hope is to help you control your power to liberate your Soul, and allow you to experience the world in the way it was meant to be.

In everyday parlance, we use the word "soul" to refer to what I experience as a force of energy that can be reduced to pure awareness. For simplicity, I will refer to this as the Soul. We use spirituality as a modality to Soul discovery. However, spirituality is a science which is constituted of the finer elements in this Universe that our civilization does not yet understand. By finer things, I mean quantum physics, and an even finer substance beyond quantum. When compared to material science, which is objective, spirituality remains a subjective science. There are visible, and therefore physical and invisible metaphysical parts of our existence. This means that science can pick up pieces of our visible Universe, physical matter, and structure processes to derive an outcome. Spirituality, on the other hand, resides in the metaphysical. It has to be experienced. There is nothing tangible to test and prove, at least not yet.

The blatant hypocrisy of material science is that it accepts gravity as one of the forces that joins both worlds. This unseen force is accepted as a physical force, not because we can see it, but because the brain can grasp the effect it has on matter. Science accepts it, and has retro equated gravity into a number to fit an equation, and we have all accepted it, and moved on. I am not disparaging science, as it is the only tool in our learning process in this university of the game called life. As a matter of fact, I know that all my experiences will be repeated by science in the near future when spirituality and science meet to create modern science. Sadly, it will not happen in my lifetime.

If one assumes that gravity, or electromagnetic forces exists, and it is not visible, this very concept should serve to demonstrate that the metaphysical exists, and is just not seen. However, do not allow this to affect the delivery of my message, because despite its subjective nature, there are many successful cultures that are built on spirituality as their very foundation. That is proof enough for us in the world of the metaphysical.

In Eastern cultures, spirituality and the journey to the Soul is embraced, nurtured, and taught. In those cultures, one can spend a whole lifetime waiting to anticipate the arrival of that Divine essence, or experiencing the Soul. While, in other cultures, like in the Western cultures, spirituality is not as well embraced. Just less than 50 years ago, some intuitive women in Salem, Massachusetts, were burned by a British witch-hunter.

The knowledge of the construct of the human body and the holographic world was well known and written about by many mystics. Many years ago, Plato told you this truth hidden in the story of Plato's cave. The truth must be embraced and understood in time to prevent the full destruction of a being called the Earth. This living creature called Earth, like us, is growing, and She is being destroyed because of our spiritual slumber, self-ignorance, and greed. I do not think that, as humans, we should remain in such ignorance. After millions of years, we fail to recognize that our body-brain complexes are in fact AI, and are vehicles.

Your body is a vehicle, created as an AI by inter-dimensional beings. You, the energy Soul that you are, is billions of years old. The avatar body has been upgraded numerous times, which we have come to call evolution. The Neanderthals, the Denisovans, and Homo sapiens are no longer around because their vehicle form became extinct. Those vehicles were outgrown and have been improved upon, resulting in us. This current version of Homo sapiens is undergoing an upgrade, and this current version of us will be extinct within the next 200 years. We are currently existing among each other in varying subtle stages of extinction and evolution.

Our vehicle engineers, the inter-dimensional beings, explained to me that I am a tagged human, and there are many of us who are tagged. I am an alien-human hybrid being. Do not be alarmed by this revelation, as we are all aliens. My design was permitted to engage certain DNA genetic methylation effects since birth which granted me telepathy. In many other humans, they are endowed with some other psionics. We are followed over the course of our lifetime to see how we use these abilities, and, in doing so, they decide to add or remove those abilities from the next version of Homo sapiens.

We can call the next version of us Homo sapiens psionics. We already have labels for these versions of ourselves, and have since called them autistic. The current culture and climate does not make it safe or acceptable for humans to admit their individual uniqueness, and so, even if they can move mountains, they will not come forward. This must change. In much the same way Mercedes-Benz upgraded my 2021 car to their 2025 version by simply tweaking the performance and adding features, that is exactly how the human vehicles are being upgraded to psionics. We all have psionics, and seamlessly use these abilities. Examine yourself so that you can identify, utilize, and enhance your abilities.

I do not want to hurt any feelings, as I am empathetic to the documented injuries, and frightening experiences of humans who have been abducted. I, too, have been abducted. But I want to point out that, when you take your car into the mechanic to get your tires rotated, the brake pads changed, or the spark plug renewed, should your car feel offended that it was pulled apart. Humans, in the name of research, tag

165

lions, zebras, monkeys, and other types of animals to learn and study them. I have had no negative experiences in my abductions, and so, I am comfortable with the fact that I am a tagged human, if that means that my sacrifice will contribute to the betterment of humanity.

When we advance in consciousness, we will be able to separate our energy signature, the Soul, from our vehicle, and not be offended by an examination or a fine tuning. The ability to disengage will enhance our Earthly experience.

The same way that not all cars are made by the same car maker, not all human vehicles are designed and managed by the same inter-dimensional beings. The energy signature of the human, the "I," came to Earth from many different regions of the Universe. For this reason, the individual interaction of an abducted human will vary.

In other words, as humans, the things we believe make up our differences, like the color of our skin, the color of our eyes, our race, or nationality are really unimportant, and only cause us to fight against ourselves. What defines us is the driver of the vehicle. Who is driving the vehicle? We are thousands of years into this civilization, and we still have not accepted our reality. We have allowed others to write us a bedtime story, similar to the emperor with no clothes, and we are now convinced that the human body is the "I." There are beings that have no vested interest for the Earth's affairs, and, hence, totally disregard the human vehicle and Soul. Others care about Earth as a being, and care about the human vehicle and Soul. This is what drives the human story of God and the Devil.

Let me briefly describe the construct of the human body. The human body has visible and invisible parts that interact with the visible and invisible forces of the Universe. The flesh body as we know it, is surrounded by an electromagnetic layer made up of a quantum force field called the mind. Surrounding that is the outermost more refined beyond the quantum energy layer called consciousness. This layer of consciousness forms a tubular track connecting to the core of the body-brain complex. The outer force fields are connected to the flesh human body by a 3D triangular electromagnetic field that is regulated by the vagus nerve on the right, and the human cardiac impulse on the left. The mind is connected to the brain via a seat around the neck and shoulders in the triangle force field. One apex of the triangle connects to the pineal gland, while the remaining two apices of the triangle correspond on the left to the heart, and on the right to the vagus nerve. The mind can disengage from the body, and consciousness can disengage from the body and the mind when the electromagnetic signal from the heart and vagus nerve is lowered to a certain threshold. Due to this design, when the human is viewed in the right way, we appear as a toroidal ball of light.

To demonstrate this design in a relatable way, I can elucidate this by saying, we can get subjective and objective information from the body. For example, we interrogate the heart using an electrocardiogram dynamically demonstrating chest pain. We examine the brain with an electrocardiogram demonstrating seizures. However, if we feel pain that is so real to us, or if we communicate love, and are bubbling in the emotion of love, neither of those can be quantified. At least not yet. This is because those emotions are not in our flesh brain, it is in the first energy layer around us called our minds. So, let me make it clear, the mind is not in the brain, it is outside of the body.

I am not going to get too technical with this book, but to quote Hermes, "as above and below, as without so within." Imagine this holographic reality as a nest of Russian dolls. The life seen within the greater Universe is reflected within the body. Each organ is its own individual entity with its own center of Soul. Each volunteered to come together to make you the vehicle. Each has its center of intelligence as manifested by the heart, the gut liver, and the brain, and these we can prove so far. All are capable of self regeneration. They work in unity, and the brain does not assume superiority because it is seated in the head. The heart does not claim preference because it manages your Soul. Down to the minute structure within each cell, they all work together within a symphony to make you. It is only humans that lack this understanding of itself in design, and its place in the order of the Universe.

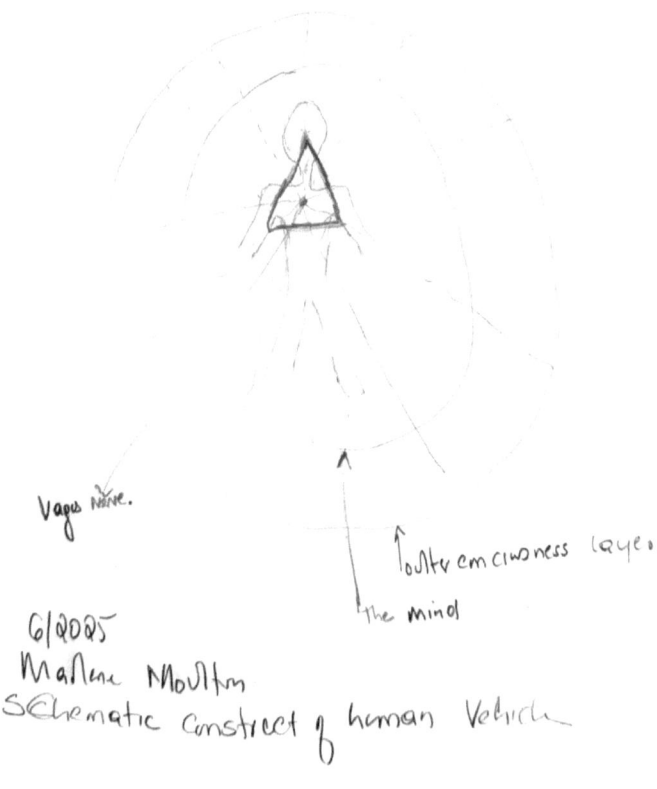

Vague Nerve.

Outer consciousness layer
the mind

6/2025
Marlene Moulton
Schematic Construct of human Vehicle

When I visualized this, and put it on the paper, I immediately thought of the Vitruvian Man. I wondered if this is what Leonardo De Vinci saw in the 1400's. I am not an artist, I am a medical doctor, and based on my personal metaphysical experiences, my perspective on the meaning of the information received is very different, though I suspect it is similar.

The blatant truth is that billions of years ago, this knowledge of the game called life, the construct, and super nature of humans and the holographic nature of reality was well known and easily accessible. Us, humans, lived in spirit, metaphysically, in the finer quantum existence more than we lived in this crystallized light called the flesh. This is because we could disengage the energy Soul from matter. This knowledge is known to mystics as our ethereal energy body and luminous self. It is why it was important to write this information in stone, because civilizations before us lost the information when the Earth was destroyed in the last nuclear cataclysm.

Today the information is known, governed, and guarded. There are those who are well aware that the human body is an AI, and has manipulated and tampered with it, and has successfully been regenerated. We call this cloning. Their inability to master quantum and energy transfer, in general, is our saving grace from making whole armies of humans. It is not far-fetched, as this was attempted by other civilizations, as seen with the 1974 discovery of Qin Shi Huang's 8000 terracotta warriors.

I will avoid physics and technicalities, as the Universe also has visible and invisible parts. We can agree on some of the invisible energy as gravity, but then there is visible tangible matter. The part of the Universe we see is grossly made up of coarse dense electrons, protons, neutrons. The parts that we cannot see are made up of finer quantum particles like quarks, and an even higher dimension made up of neutrinos. I am able to walk through mountains, rocks or walls in other dimensions, and still feel the effects of the object on my body as I walk through them. In the same way the black triangular UFO craft I encountered was able to interact with the environment leaving behind no sound, no heat through friction, and did not affect the trees or wires in its path. We each have to learn how to stabilize the neutrinos to create material that can be manifested and utilized for creation in this dimension. This stabilizing force is the mind in you, and is the bridge to the next dimension, if you will.

There are rules of engagement for how to use the forces of the mind to manipulate via light to create, manifest, and heal ourselves. This very special truth was utilized as intended for billions of years. Imagine a system in which we are born, educated, and nurtured by our families who encourage us to embrace the energy part of your being, and its intuition known as the Souls. We then learn how to navigate the body-brain complex, and its five senses. With that support behind us, we transition into practices to further empower the Soul.

By the time we get to formal education, we move on to integrating intuitions into the body-brain complex at a very early age. We learn how to use the ego to our advantage in the process of creation in the game of life. We also create families, business, art, music, and everything else in between. If and when we need to engage in medicine because we are sick, we are taught how to heal ourselves using regeneration techniques, energy force fields, sounds, plants, and animal based foods. In the event that fails, we resort to what man has designed for extreme situations; medicine. Finally, imagine a government that supports all that, too. No, it is not my naive imagination, and this is not utopia. This is what existed before it was assaulted by dark forces of the infrastructures we created: religion, education, government, and medicine. But it was religion that led to the onslaught to kill knowledge and truth.

During the Dark Ages, the dominant religious church sought to wipe this truth from the face of the Earth by killing everyone who spoke of it. The Cathars and the Essenes were a living proof to this fact, as both cultures were destroyed by acts of genocide by the same church. They were upholding and practicing living in the spirit, while utilizing their consciousness to raise awareness that we were all energy and light.

Similarly, Giordano Bruno suffered at the hands of the church for this truth. Africans continue to suffer because of this truth. Africans, as both a culture and people, have lived in harmony with the Universe, and respected the presence of inter-dimensional beings. The beings taught, loved, and shared with and cared for them. African cultures are of one understanding that the Divine essence is in all things.

The Westerners misunderstood the people they encountered in Africa, but recognized the power of their practice; their ignorance drove fear into their hearts. Their odd ways were perceived as backwards and uneducated, and the story of witches was born. Led by the British, a massive campaign to reform and to educate Africa began, and has continued to this day. There was a mass attempt to eradicate the spirit under the disguise of the slave trade of the Africans, dispensing them all over the world in an attempt to annihilate their "God." But the African God never died, and the plan backfired.

The attempt to assault the Divine used the African slave trade to take the spiritism of the true Divine in all corners of the Earth. Later, and with the right knowledge, the spirit of truth found everyone, not just Africans, because the Divine is not owned by anyone; it is our humanness. However, when it was later accepted, it was blended into Western and European cultures and buried into secret societies. The information is no secret; you do not need to be initiated or knighted to discover yourself.

Without diverging, in the same vein that the dark forces believed that this spirit resided in Africans, to this day, they have one primary goal: to eradicate Africans and the miracle and contribution of Africa and Africans from history. The contribution of Africans to humanity, and the special miracle they hold in the process of creation and of the vehicle called the human body, cannot be erased. There is a special lineage of Africans from the stars, Sirius, Orion, and Alpha Centauri that are of the original mitochondrial DNA that has been tracked through all humans present in the original human vehicle, and always will be. It cannot be erased, and, yes, it was first in female form. It is the original blueprint for the human, the best, most amazing engineering software ever made. It designed secrets protected by a galactic force, and its makers never left. They reserve the power to materialize and dematerialize, and in a few years, you will remember I told you so.

The dark forces, armed by the Romans, utilized the political force called the Catholic Church to seize and burn the books in which the truth of humanity was written. Leaving behind religion, the invisible force was that of mind control. When the truth became a treasured secret, and was buried for safety, humans were separated from this knowledge, and overtime, was led by the ignorant campaign orchestrated by a few who partnered with beings whose only motivation was greed.

They are still present, living right alongside us, campaigning to keep us ignorant, and sell us our capabilities wrapped up in fancy technologies. What I love most about truth is it cannot be erased, and all of our history and the truth still resides in the other dimension permanently recorded and alive. Every version of it. The holographic Universe, like a giant computer history book of truth, keeps every version of our world and actions in all other dimensions.

You are told that angels watch and record your actions for some holy day of judgement. Most people know this place of truth as the Akashic

173

record, and it can be accessed like a library where you can walk into it and view it. Ask any other out-of-body traveller if it is true. When the truth about humans and the holographic world was hidden in this dimension, it was not secured in one piece, lest it be rediscovered, seized, and permanently destroyed. In the process of its protection, this secret knowledge was eventually broken into many parts and hidden in the four corners of the Earth. The information was hidden in plain sight in all the different cultural practices to become a whisper of mouth to ears.

As our civilization progresses and broadens in consciousness, the truth is re-emerging blowing in the wind. The wind is the spoken word that will be uttered in the culture in which it finds itself. Therefore, in Eastern philosophy, the information is delivered in Buddhism, Taoism, or Hinduism. In Western philosophy, it speaks via Christianity and all its varying Protestant forms. In the Southern hemispheres, like in African cultures, it will continue to live in the Dogan tribe, and in the stories told from mouth to ears. In the Northern hemisphere, like Nordic or Celtic cultures, it will also live. The culture in which you find yourself is how the pieces of the puzzle will speak to you.

It is our responsibility to experience the truth, not to be told or preached to from a pulpit, and asked to have faith. Many of those who speak from high places have never experienced the living Divine or the miracle of their humanness. They are locked and bound in the darkness of ignorance that they are thoughtlessly delivering, in an attempt to try to convince you that you are weak, or lacking in greatness. They try to teach you to pray while you remain the prey. The very act of prayer engages you in a negative vibrational state the moment you seek out someone else to provide the blessings and abundance that already reside in you. When you acknowledge your own power, it will begin to operate from a place of strength in the mind as a state of knowing, as you command or instruct the Universe to materialize your needs, and it will.

It is our responsibility to not judge any organized religions, but to remain open-minded with prudence and understanding. Do not be a prisoner of your religious dogma, learn to question even your own religion, be a little curious, and investigate other cultures and religions so that you can pull truth buried within the fluff. Please remember that many eons ago, the writers, those sages and teachers, were risking their lives to deliver the truth to you, and, so, it is sometimes coded and covered in layers. Christ consciousness is one such truth, because of its layers, it is riddled with parables that need interpretation and explanation. Christos is light, it is energy, and it is you.

Awakening to this truth of the illusion of this world must be experienced, not believed. In this illusion, faith is the first step, and many have taken the first step, and never moved past it. It is this inertia that has allowed the individual Soul to be captured in the slavery of the external energy search, and is constantly relinquishing its powers.

Let us examine the game changer, and what led to the concealment and protection of the truth. In many ways, it is us, humans, who turned on ourselves. The enlightened Soul has a will, and that will, when used for low vibration and self service, is deadly. The infrastructures namely, government, education, religion, and medicine, as previously discussed, exist to guide our Souls in the early years to develop the self, or the ego, if you will. Then, in the later years, it exists to guide us to find our Soul. Some of the players in this game of life utilized the wild card called the will, and powerfully mixed in negative invisible forces in a selfish game of greed, which led to slavery of other players in the game of life. Their strategic forces were enforced by the infrastructures we created billions of years ago to build a civilization. With this, the dark forces have the players brainwashed. They have weaponized our instinct to seek internal energy, to seek the Soul, and are using it against us. The infrastructures have managed to convince us that humans, the light man, made of light and energy, experience a stir inside of us that should be used for seeking energy outside of ourselves.

This propaganda is what is used by the education system to keep our children intensely focused on the individual self, the ego, but never teach about the Soul and intuition. Education fails us by redirecting all efforts into self-development, missing the early and most powerful years of psionic development. In those youthful years, we retain the strongest relationship with our Soul, and the Divine. This innate awareness in us is driven out by fear and competition, and is totally reprogrammed to something deeply focused on the self, our ego, and the external world. If politics can be removed from our educational system, the focus on the Soul can be restored.

Religion has flipped the narrative by removing God from our temple, then charging us to access God. Religion tells us that we are looking for God, something that sounds so much greater than you, but you are actually searching for yourself. If your body is the temple of God, why are you not digging inside your temple to find God? Hold on to your dollar power, and remember that what you are seeking is inside you, and it is free. All it takes is time, time to slow down, breathe, and meditate.

The institution of medicine, my own profession, fails to educate us about our true nature. This infrastructure reinforces our ignorance because of greed. Medicine is a huge part of our financial slavery; it exchanges our dollar power for the "pill for that cure." Medicine has confined humans just to the body, and believes that the mind resides in the brain. They teach us that humans are a pound of flesh, but you are not that. We have lived in ignorance, trained in ignorance, and have operated in ignorance. Many meta-physical doctors know the truth of our being, and are working hard to change the paradigm.

Be more informed, and be aware that medicine markets to your fears; fears of getting sick, fears of pain when you are sick, fears of growing old, and fears of death. I can go on, but you get the picture. There is a pill for all these fears. Yet we spend all our money on pills for sickness, pain and aging, and spend the most on preventing death. In the end, you will still get sick, you still feel pain when you are sick, you will still grow old, and you will die. Either way, you are out of money. Hold on to your dollar power knowing that your Soul experiences none of these things your body does. The eternal energy recognizes that you never age, and you never truly die.

The age of our own designed artificial intelligence, AI, is coming, and soon my profession, as a medical industrial complex, will be in a whole scheme to further disempower us. Soon, we will be offered AI parts that make us superhuman, but do not fall for it. We are already superhuman.

The government remains the most corrupt of all the infrastructures. Despite the nature of corruption and poor governing skills, we need a government. When Jesus flipped the tables in the temple, it was not to imply that government was not needed, but to remind us that it must be operated with fairness and integrity. But sadly, the government uses its facilities to enforce all the other improper operations of the other infrastructures.

Even after finding our Souls, we are not going to hijack some matrix, or escape the matrix, as some say. We will still be living here, carrying on the growth of our Souls. But we must be able to see through the illusion in order to succeed at our vignette lessons when they present themselves. Like I said, it is all about the growth of our Souls, and so, in the process of learning, we create. When we started sharing our creations and energy with each other, we developed a fair platform called money. This was how the illusion of the Earth school was hijacked. Instead of sharing, it became an entire scheme for us to relinquish our financial power. It is all about money. The money we earn is delivered back into the system, and we are brainwashed into doing so voluntarily. We are doing so spiritually asleep, while trapped in a bond of material slavery.

This hijacked version of the holographic game of life has us spellbound, forgetting ourselves, forgetting the stars that we came from, and forgetting the original true source, the Divine. Our infrastructures have become comfortable with our state of ignorance at the financial expense of the human race, as a collective. They will go to great lengths, and at all expense to keep the status quo. But energy cannot be created, and neither can it be destroyed. It will keep rising.

The dark force game changers have failed to see the impending doom in their system, and the potential destruction to the Earth. When the infrastructures implemented its system, we became brainwashed and reprogrammed from our innate stir to search for the energy within, and chose to search for the energy without. The Earth suffers because they cannot see the Earth as themselves. Falsely, they think the Earth does not feel, think, see or have the essence of the Divine. They just keep trampling. The Earth has trees that are to us, her lungs, she has the Sun like we have a heart. But our ignorance has cajoled us to spend our whole life destroying the Earth in search of energy. Collectively, we search for energy in the form of carbon as oil, coal, and gas, hydro-energy from our waters, turbo energy from wind turbines, solar from our Sun, and the most threatening of all, nuclear energy from the elements.

As discussed, we have all bought into the programing that humans, made of pure energy, need something outside of the avatar self, called, "energy" in order to live. Do not be so quick to say you do not search for those types of energy, because, individually, we search for energy sometimes as emotions of love in our search for creating families, or energy as material goods to constitute the external search.

Your natural instincts to seek stirs in the mind, creates a desire turned inside out, and has manifested as all manners of addictions to external things. It has led to addictions including drugs, alcohol, sex, food, and love. From where we sit, we cannot yet see this, therefore, grant yourself some grace. The propaganda is designed to nullify all manifestations of the external search for energy, hence their inability to fulfill you. But nothing outside of you will ever fulfill you.

You "need" nothing outside of yourself except for food and water, which was already provided to you for free by our gracious host—the Earth. You are to use the force of wind, water, and fire to generate food, a bi-product of your creation, to sustain the body-brain avatar's requirements in order to allow it to regenerate. The natural surroundings provide food, which allows you to enjoy the game with many more days of rest than you currently have. These rest days allow you to find time for

179

self-discovery. Our creations must cause no danger to ourselves and others, and be used for experiences that are not "needs."

Instead, we are slaves to our desires, and our own instincts have trapped us in the "labor of love" concept. We find ourselves working more, with two or three jobs, with no time for ourselves. We are doing this "work" creation process with no balance of rest or time for the self-discovery uniquely designed to have you avoid meditation

The "work" then generates a "reward" money that we can then exchange for energy. External energy can be groceries, clothes, shoes, cars, houses, or even healthcare services. So, with all the power of money we earned, we have exchanged it for carbon goods; yes, that source of external energy. We gave away our power. This distraction by labour with no balance or rest was designed to keep us with no time to meditate or be silent in order to start our journey to the Soul.

When this distraction was not enough, days of rest were created for us to hand over our money. Days filled with the distraction of marketing packed activities concealed as holidays like Christmas, Easter, Valentine's Day, and even Labor Day. During these holidays, we volunteer to be relieved of our hard-earned money in exchange for trivial external energy, or "goods." This only stirs up emotions of temporary satisfaction.

We are the energy that this game is trying to bury. We need to play this game back to our Soul. You are an amazing superhuman, made of pure energy locked in crystalized matter searching for energy. Time is of the essence for your discovery, and, as a collective, we need to wake up to our Souls.

But first, we must break free of the external search by knowing ourselves within. You must recognize that the energy which you are searching for is inside of you. In doing so, you can break free from the collective search for energy in the external world. Hold on to your dollar power, as the only people who will suffer are the ones who constructed the propaganda. Until we are awake, we will live our days on this Earth spiritually asleep, wrapped within a dream of slavery.

This slavery is one created by dark forces that saw something outside of itself that was greater, more magnificent, and miraculous, and called it God. Those forces are of this world and continue to live right alongside you. Though those forces may create havoc on humanity, they are also miraculous in the way they continue to inspire, lead, and hold power over matter.

In the end, you will discover that you, too, have power over matter; power to walk directly through the mountains, fly though the sky, or rain fire on this Earth, if you choose. Do not be afraid of those dark forces because nothing can hurt your Soul. They cannot inhabit you or hurt you because they are not "Gods." What matters is knowing that your Divine consciousness, the real God, lives inside you.

In this journey, not only is the veil of the illusion of separateness lifted, but it allows us to look beyond the veil and into the root cause of the illusion that is also clear. The story of us humans was retold and rewritten in an attempt to bury the Divine fact that we are all super powerful multi-dimensional beings; spirits of light operating in an avatar body-brain vehicle as flesh. The story of our purpose, my purpose, and your purpose, is being stifled by a story that is currently being told; a story that is very far from the truth. You know the story, and the storytellers, as they are cloaked in all types of religious practices. I am not here to add to useless wars, but to bring your Soul peace. In doing so, I hope to assist you and all of us to create a more peaceful multi-dimensional world with the power of our minds.

Do you remember how I was viscerally triggered by war? At the time, I could not pinpoint the reason. Over time, and with greater clarity, the truth took me to my knees. I want you to find your Soul because, in time, you, too will see what I have seen, and no words will be needed. Speaking like an orchid, it is through the power of silence and not using words to give power to that darkness that will eradicate it. What I mean is silence of the mind via meditation. Just like the plants who do not speak, but do so for the right person, the right words on the wrongs ears can cause war. I can hear you say, "just tell me." But let me remind you that our human eyes are limited, and that we are not alone in this Universe.

Learn how to play the game and learn to enact actions that force the darkness to respect your presence and power. Practice days of financial protests, let us all choose one day each month when we purchase nothing, no food, no material goods. Then watch the impact on the economy in one day. Soon, we can add one additional day to that protest then eventually one week. Stay off the streets, keep your placards at home. I have lived for many years, and that approach has done very little for humanity, except get us abused and killed. Resort to your true nature of contentment, and let us learn how to not spend, one day at a time.

There are very strong negative forces here, and some of those negative forces are exercised through us, humans. Yes, even us humans who were granted grace to succeed through the illusion of the Earth school. But once they tasted the power, they aligned themselves with other "players," or "students" in the game of life's university to the detriment of us humans who were still spiritually asleep. This paradigm is what is being covered up at all costs, because it can only survive if you remain asleep.

The Universe has a grand plan in the game of life, and she also has forces that are seen and unseen. The God I know is truly omnipotent, and therefore powerful; omniscient, and is capable of seeing all things; and omnipresent, with the power to exist everywhere. God is awareness, and all things are aware. We all have our own unique awareness signature vibrations. The signature vibration of the Divine God is love. When you experience your Soul, your intuitive sense of feeling will confirm this fact.

I say all this to say that the God I met and know is not hateful, vengeful, ostracising, spiteful or promotes wars. All these vibrations are negative vibrations, and are the opposite of God. The opposite of who you are deep inside, and you know it. If you live in the true signature of God's love, you would not need moral laws to remind you not to kill, hate or steal because you understand that all those actions are committed against yourself, not against others.

In our modern day, we have gone so far off course, yet the same infrastructures are playing the same game with different players, which is putting us in greater blinding distress. The Earth, in her growth, responds to electromagnetic forces, so solar flares will come fast, furious, and fierce just like us. The infrastructures will try to convince you that it is your fault, triggered by global warming. The electromagnetic energy that the Sun discharges disrupts the status quo and the natural energy, that you, the real you, the man made of electromagnetic energy and light will respond to, and begin to decode and up-code. This is nothing that our infrastructures can stop, thank goodness. It will happen regardless of if you are ready or not. I just want you to not be caught off guard. You will begin to notice changes within yourself, so be cautious who you seek help from, because you may find yourself pegged by the infrastructure. If you are not aware of the possibility of these changes, when they happen to you, you may think that you are sick in mind, body or both. With the wrong help, you can find yourself buried deeper in the external search by the "pill for that cure."

Do not remain ignorant of the process as this is the awakening that many cultures speak of. If we can find our way back to our Soul, your time here on Earth will be so beautiful. Magical, even. You can open your eyes in the mornings, with the positive vibration of gratitude; not the negative vibration of prayers (the act of begging). You can begin to sing songs of praise like Solomon, and write poetry of love like David in Psalms. You can live in the flow with the Universe; not with rigid plans. You, the creator, can begin to create and share your energy freely with the signature of love. Together, we can begin to live freely.

I am not here to teach you how to manifest. Forget simple manifesting, and grab hold of the rules of the game to wake up to the real you. Because when you do, I am sure that you will walk away understanding that manifesting material things is not something you will want to even bother with, unless it is to enrich the lives of others. There is a much bigger world out there to be discovered in the unseen magical invisible Universe. The word manifesting is a representation of man's infestation of the Earth. Like a virus, our incessant material desire has left the Earth covered in a litter of garbage. There are many enlightened Souls out here grabbing your attention by teaching you how to manifest. They are unaware that their own actions contribute to the disease.

Just also remember, life is a game in which we are here in a giant play collecting data for reasons we do not know. So, do not take it so seriously or to the detriment of self and others. Enjoy the Soul seeking process, create beautiful things, and linger in the beauty of the complex platform called Earth, which was designed to give us this illusion of reality. It is just a university, a place of learning with each lesson wrapped up as a vignette.

Do not forget that Shakespeare reminded us that this world is but a stage. Remember, while you are inhabiting the body-brain avatar, love hard and laugh a lot because in the end, it is only the memories that we created, good or bad, that we leave with. So strive to create good ones. Our Souls will need it for the next step in our journey.

I hope my delivery was effective and that you clearly comprehend this university called the Universe. I hope that you grasp the concept of the holographic world, and the lesson in the game called life. Above all, I hope that you can see that you are not only playing for your Soul, but you are playing for its freedom. Never forget that the real you is an energy, and is a part of the Divine. You were never created and, therefore, cannot be destroyed. You were not born, your body is not you. Your Soul is sagacious, omnipotent, and omniscient, so go play this game, and unapologetically start winning.

Chapter 13:

FINDING YOUR GODSELF

Now that you understand my journey, I can hear you asking so how can I help you on your journey to within. It appears that, once you identify even one seemingly odd thing in this illusionary world, it gets the ball rolling. Please remember that I am still on this journey, and it is never ending. I am not a guru, and have no desire to be one. But if my words can help you to remember, or ignite a fire to power your search, I would have done my part. I can tell you one thing, the key to your own discovery is waiting. If I were to lay it all out, here is how I would start.

Love:

Loving yourself is not narcissism, it is self-love. By first loving yourself, you will be able to go through this process and learn to love everyone else. Give yourself grace in the process, and refrain from judgement or the shortcomings of yourself that are trying to find your Soul. It was through the overwhelming vibration of love that overtook me, and made me realize that I was in the presence of the Divine.

The Ultimate powerful Divine energy inside you loves you just as you are; that unique part of your being that is quirky and funny, short or tall. That is what makes you so very special. Stick with being yourself, and know that being anyone else is not as exciting. Of all the things that we can do, love is the most important. Be kind to everything, the animate and the inanimate, and remember that in doing this, you are being kind to yourself. Remember, you cannot take anything with you, and it is how you treat yourself and others in this game called life that can speed up or delay your progress to your Soul.

Who am I?

After loving yourself enough to want to find the rest of yourself, start asking, "Who am I?" I strongly believe that the Universe wants you to know yourself, and what is waiting for you is the knock on the door of the Universe. This simple question, "Who am I?" is the key. When asked with sincerity and curiosity, it seems to be the invitation to enter.

Meditate:

Finding your Soul starts and ends with meditation. Through meditation, you will begin to quiet your mind. Meditation that requires us to lay still and be quiet is great, but the practice of being present is much easier to grow the Soul. Be present. Stop multitasking. Begin living in the moment by paying attention to what you are doing, and doing it slowly. Remember that you are a human being, and all you have to do is just be. Be present in the now, not yesterday or tomorrow. That is all that is important in the game. It is through this practice that you will begin to not trust your eyes and emotions, just observe them. Be mindful because the person you fail to acknowledge may have a message for you. Find time to connect with nature, and see the Divine in everything that you do.

Create:

Once you are present, begin to create. You are a creator, so never stop creating, but, instead, balance this with rest, and meditation. Understanding the force of the spoken words is powerful. Remember, it is the wind that is interacting with the Ether, and it is another very fast way to create. The force creates a vibration in the Ether, and interacts with the invisible parts of both the Universe and the other players to affect your desire. It is a visible force, so use it wisely. Speak with authority, and always with positivity.

Journal:

Human memory is very fleeting, so keep a journal. Write down your dreams, as, in many cases, they can be a message to you, or even insight into your past or future life. Use it to play for the freedom of your Soul.

If you take nothing away from what I am about to share with you about this game called life, learn this: your Soul lives when you are asleep. When you open your eyes in the morning, you are in the school of Earth, learning many lessons through a structured game called life. The main objective is to discover your Soul in a process that ignites the spark sleeping inside you. Remember, it is an energy source that is plugged into an unlimited supply of consciousness. This is what you are supposed to be seeking in your spiritual search.

Believe me, you are an intense energy, and an amazing ray of light. From infinity to form, from light to the crystalized light called matter, I have lived it. You are the Divine projection, and you are part of something grander and more beautiful. You are here to experience duality, but you are not dual. Your experience of duality, and your ability to exercise the will to choose love and all that is good is what this school is about. To demonstrate this through many different vignettes shows you that you have the power to transmute emotions and stay in a positive vibration. You are the Source of the Divine God, but you are buried, and you are lost. You must discover yourself, and only then can you truly start living.

When I discovered myself, my purpose for the remainder of the days that I will spend here on Earth drastically changed. I hope that my journey gives you courage, and reinforces whatever stage of your journey you find yourself. If you have not yet started, make that first step. The Universe is waiting for your permission to begin.

www.ingramcontent.com/pod-product-compliance
Lightning Source LLC
Chambersburg PA
CBHW021630120626
46545CB00002B/482